Powerful devotional
readings based on

THE SERMON ON
THE MOUNT

First...
the
Kingdom

Edited by
Thomas A. Jones
and Sheila Jones

Discipleship
PUBLICATIONS INTERNATIONAL

One Merrill Street
Woburn, MA 01801
1-800-727-8273
Fax (617) 937-3889

Acknowledgements

Our thanks to Jerri Newman, our able editorial assistant, for her heart and hard work and to Nora Robbins, DPI's talented art director, for the cover design. Also thanks to Scott Vigneault who worked late nights on the format and typesetting and to Chris Costello, a talented artist, whose work is found on the front and back covers. Most of all we continue to give thanks to God whose grace will enable us to live the message of this book.

The Editors

First...the Kingdom

ISBN 1-884553-16-8

Dedication

To George Gurganus who disdained comfort and ease and lived until the very end seeking first the Kingdom of God, and to his wife Irene who still amazes us with her Kingdom-first heart.

Contents

Warning

MOST BOOKS BEGIN WITH A PREFACE. WE BEGIN THIS ONE WITH A warning. The contents of this book are dangerous. The things you will find here are a threat to both the nice religious life and the secular view of the world.

Many years ago I heard someone say that the worst sin in teaching the Bible is to make it seem boring. An equally strong statement needs to be made about writing about the Bible. God forbid that we should publish another boring little book about some biblical idea. God forbid that we should ask you to engage in more bland religious tedium.

One thing Jesus was not was boring. He walked into a town and things started to happen. He got a crowd together on a hillside, and when he was done, the place was abuzz. What he taught shook the place up.

If this book fails to shake people up, we will have failed in our task. The sermon on which it is based shook people to the core. It rattled the cages. It sent shock waves through the crowds. Every defender of the *status quo* surely found most of it to be dangerous. That sermon and this book are not about a mild injection of religion, but about a radical, from the inside-out change of heart, character and priorities. The challenge here will send tremors into your life, but if you embrace the summons, you will find something most people only dream about.

If you are determined not to be shook up—if you are committed to staying right where you are—put this book away. Recycle it. Use it for kindling, or better yet, give it to someone with a different attitude. But whatever you do, don't read it.

On the other hand, if you want a new perspective, a new paradigm, a new set of principles that are so right that they will bring you life, read on. If the truth of God scares you to death but you want it anyway because you know it is right, stay with us. We don't think you will be disappointed.

T.A.J.

Prologue to the Climb

"TURN THE OTHER CHEEK." "LOVE YOUR ENEMIES." "DO NOT LET the left hand know what the right hand is doing." "Be perfect." "Do not judge." "Seek first the Kingdom of God." "Do to others as you would have them do to you." Just some of the words from what is still the most radical sermon ever preached. Known around the world as the Sermon on the Mount, it is a biblical Mount Everest, rising high above normal ethics, religion and spirituality. To stand at its base and contemplate living its message humbles every heart that sees it clearly. To actually leave the security of the flatlands and climb toward its peak is to embark on a journey that can only be completed by the receiving of abundant grace.

Many are those who will pay lip service to its loftiness and grandeur, but few are those who believe its message can be lived in the modern world. Fewer still are those who will commit themselves to follow it with all their hearts. Preferring a broader way—a much safer and less demanding way—the "many" will turn away from this narrow path that tests our resolve, determination and spiritual conviction. So taught Jesus in the sermon itself.

This, however, is a book for the other group Jesus described. It is not for the "many" but for the "few"—those few who will take the greatest challenge, those few who will abandon themselves to the will of God though it looks like an impossible calling.

There are no physical or intellectual requirements for this expedition. One does not have to be blessed with self-confidence, self-esteem, creativity or high energy to tackle this challenge. (Isn't this good to know?) As Jesus makes clear in the first moment of the message, only those who realize their utter inadequacy have a chance of making it. What is needed is not smarts or looks or sinews but spiritual allegiance. This sermon and this book about the sermon are for those who dare to trust God and will keep trusting God and keep trusting God. Along the journey they will be called fools and fanatics. But in the end they will have no regrets, for while others weep and gnash their teeth, they will know every blessing the sermon promises.

If you are eager for the greatest of challenges that brings the greatest rewards, here are a few other things to keep in mind as you go with us into the heart of this message:

1. These are the words of Jesus Christ. The Sermon on the Mount is so contrary to what we have learned in the world that there will be times when something inside us will fight against what we are hearing. But we must remember whose words these are. These are the words of the Alpha and the Omega, he who was in the beginning with God, he who was God. In a book called *Understanding the Sermon on the Mount* Harvey McArthur has a chapter on 12 different ways people interpret the sermon. He says he could have called this chapter "Versions and Evasions of the Sermon on the Mount" because 11 of the 12 give "reasonable explanations" why you really don't have to do what the sermon says. We will all be tempted to come up with some of those ourselves, but remember these are the words of Jesus Christ.

2. This is a message for all of us. At one time Roman Catholic theology taught that some of the teachings here were only for certain monastic orders. Protestants later said the things here were just to make us realize how badly we needed grace. But both of these views are wrong as Jesus makes clear by the way the sermon ends: *"Therefore everyone who hears these words of mine and puts them into practice is like a wise man who built his house on the rock."* Jesus clearly is teaching these things so people would do them. Only those who put them into practice are wise.

3. Every word here is spoken out of Jesus' love and wisdom. In a bookstore one day I perused a book by a well-known psychologist. A line referring to the Sermon on the Mount caught my attention. "Jesus Christ had no right to tell people to do such a thing," wrote the highly regarded counselor. Convinced that what Jesus was asking was harmful to people, he virtually demanded that Jesus apologize for at least one of his extreme statements. Such religion, he felt, was a burden to people. The psychologist was misunderstanding two things: (1) his very limited view from his own little brain and (2) the wisdom and love of Jesus Christ behind every word in this sermon. What is here may challenge us, but it will ultimately bless us.

4. The Beatitudes are at the beginning for a reason—an important reason. The opening 12 verses are not just an italicized poetic introduction. They say something and they say something powerful. In fact, everything else in the sermon flows from these Beatitudes. Miss their message and you are in trouble. The Beatitudes are the ABC's. You learn them first and then you take them with you from that point on. Forget them and you will flounder. Without these attitudes and without a continual renewal of them, you have no chance of living this sermon. Trying to live Matthew 5-7 without the Beatitudes firmly in place is like trying to go up Mount Everest without your hiking boots. Take all the time you need here. Don't go on until these are in your heart.

5. The Sermon on the Mount is more than the words of Jesus. It is the life of Jesus. He had been living this message before he ever preached it, and after he preached it, he kept living it. To see the heart of this sermon is to see the heart of Jesus. As disciples, our basic goal is to be like Jesus, to model ourselves after him in every way. To see what that means read and medidate on this sermon.

THERE HAS NEVER BEEN A MESSAGE LIKE THIS ONE. The Sermon on the Mount is to religious thinking what the cross of Christ is to human effort. It towers above the best that men and women have to offer. But like the cross, when it is lived, it will be loved or hated. It is a double-edged sword, threatening and frightening to those who fight against it but helping and healing to those who submit to its call. Families will be divided over it. Families will be transformed by it. Some families will first be divided by it and then later transformed by it.

But one thing is for sure, this sermon will neither generate change nor controversy until there are those who will dare to put it into practice. Shut up in the covers of a book lying politely on a coffee table or almost hidden on a shelf, it will do nothing to change the world. But when even a *few* throw off their fear or their pride or whatever else holds them back, put on the gear of grace and start up the mountain, the world will feel the impact. It did 2,000 years ago and it will again.

T.A.J.

Part 1

Attitude

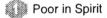

Poverty and the Good Life

"Blessed are the poor in spirit, for theirs is the kingdom of heaven" (Matthew 5:3).

J ESUS WAS FULL OF SURPRISES. HOW DO YOU BEGIN A SERMON designed to draw people into a vision of changing the world? How do you get people to believe that they can be the salt and the light that makes all the difference in the lives of others? Surely not by telling them how bad they are. Right? Surely not by saying something that causes people to feel broken and full of need. Right? Wrong, according to Jesus. (No wonder modern psychology has so much trouble with him.)

When Jesus began this earth-shaking message, he got right to the point. The people who are going to be blessed and find the Kingdom of God, the people who can live out the rest of this sermon, are those who fully understand their poverty of spirit—those who look at their own lives and their own sinfulness and freely confess, "I need help."

Spiritual Beggars

There were two words for "poor" in the Greek language. One meant poor in the sense of not owning any property. The other meant so poor that you had to beg. Guess which one is used here. That's right. Jesus says in effect, "Those who will be blessed by God are those who realize that they are spiritually and morally bankrupt and understand that before God they are spiritual beggars."

There is a powerful and essential spiritual principle here that is often missed because we want to miss it. We are in sin. God is not. We are in need. God has plenty. We can get out of our sin and have our need met only through confession and humility—only by owning up to where we really are and what condition we are really in. But once we do that, how things change. Suddenly those who are beggars have everything. Theirs is the Kingdom of God!

The Only Door

Every person who walks with God and knows God must have this experience. There is nothing optional about it. There is no way into the Kingdom except through this door.

David came in through this door. Again and again in the Psalms this King of Israel, this man who conquered his enemies and ushered in a golden age for his nation describes himself as a poor and needy man who sees he can do nothing without God. *"This poor man called, and the Lord heard him; he saved him out of all his troubles"* (34:6). *"Yet I am poor and needy; may the Lord think of me. You are my help and my deliverer; O my God, do not delay"* (40:17). *"For I am poor and needy, and my heart is wounded within me"* (109:22). Modern thinkers would say he needed to feel better about himself. God said, "That is a man after my own heart," and he blessed him and worked powerfully in his life.

Isaiah came in through this door. Seeing the awesome reality of God when he came to the temple, he cried out, *"Woe to me! I am ruined! For I am a man of unclean lips, and I live among a people of unclean lips, and my eyes have seen the King, the Lord Almighty"* (Isaiah 6:5). Not exactly what people want when they go to the crystal cathedrals of our age to be told how good they are. But God forgave all his sin and sent him out on a mission that filled his life with purpose.

Though we know little about Mary, we know she too came through this door. Why was she picked to give birth to the Savior? Because she already knew how much she needed God as her savior and she was already in a humble state before him, deeply appreciating her need for his mercy (see her song in Luke 1:46-55).

Without a doubt Paul came through this door. It took a jolt on the road to Damascus and three days of blindness and fear, but he finally came to see his poverty of spirit as clearly as any man ever saw it. *"I know that nothing good lives in me, that is, in my sinful nature,"* he wrote openly in the midst of his greatest theological treatise (Romans 7:18). *"I am the least of the apostles and do not even deserve to be called an apostle . . .But by the grace of God I am what I am,"* he told one of the churches he had planted (1 Corinthians 15:9-10). He never got too mature to talk like this. He continued to confess his poverty of spirit to the very end (1 Timothy 1:12-15, 2 Timothy 1:8-12). Leaders take note.

The Pharisee and the Tax Collector

We see this principle in the lives of real biblical people, but perhaps no one teaches us more about it than a fictional character in one of Jesus' parables (Luke 18:9-14). *"Two men went up to the temple to pray,"* says Jesus. One, a Pharisee, essentially said, "I thank you, God, that I am good man—not like these sinners. Look at all my accomplishments." The other a tax collector, in essence said, "I don't deserve to be here. God have mercy on me, a sinner." One was rich in spirit—his own. One was poor and needy. They had only one thing in common—they both went home. One went back to his house lost. The other went to bed that night justified before God and ready, if he died, to enter the gates of Heaven! By this point you know which was which.

There are many who think that they are Christians because they have committed themselves to certain ethical standards and to various church activities. But they are not Christians at all because they have never seen the magnitude of their sin and the greatness of their need. They have never felt nor acknowledged poverty of spirit. They are much more like the Pharisee than the tax collector.

Writing about this is humbling indeed. It is easy for me to say, "I thank you, God, that I see *my* sin and *my* need. I thank you that I am not like the Pharisees I see around me in the world and sometimes in the church." And suddenly I realize that with such a prayer, *I am one*. God, be merciful to me, a sinner. My sin catches me coming and going. Without you I can truly do nothing.

The Key to Everything Else

This first beatitude is the key to everything else you will read in this book. We, with our resources, cannot live this sermon. We cannot be convicted enough, committed enough or determined enough to make it happen. Only as we continue to confess to God our poverty of spirit can *his* Spirit fill us and empower us.

If you have not already noticed it, you will see that this sermon has a way of driving you back again and again to this beatitude. You will fail to have a pure heart or to forgive your brother. Lust will be in your heart. You will struggle with loving your enemy. You will lash back rather than turn the other cheek. You will self-righteously judge someone else. You will get anxious. But don't despair and don't give up. This is one time when it is all right to come back to square one. And each time you do, you will find again that there is great blessing in admitting to God the greatness of your need.

Amazing grace. The New Testament is full of it. Even the challenging Sermon on the Mount begins with it. Jesus preaches that God does nothing less than give the entire Kingdom with all its benefits and privileges to a bunch of beggars. The only catch is that *you have to admit that you are one.* You have to confess that you don't know what you are doing and that you have an absolutely tremendous need for God and his help. Does this describe you? Is it the way others would describe you? Most importantly, is this the way God would describe you?

Once this is your heart, you are off and running. In the very act of admitting your weakness and poverty, you become strong and rich. *"Yours is the Kingdom!"*

THOMAS A. JONES
Concord, Mass.

FOR FURTHER STUDY:

Job 42:1-6, 10-12
Psalm 51:1-12
Isaiah 6:1-11
Luke 18:9-14
1 Corinthians 15:1-11

A Bright New Mourning

"Blessed are those who mourn, for they will be comforted" (Matthew 5:4).

W ITH REDDENED AND SWOLLEN EYES THEY WATCH— uncomprehendingly. A last song at the graveside brings more tears. It's incredibly hard to say good-bye to one you love, to one who holds a large chunk of your life within his or her own. The hurt cuts deep. The heaviness in the heart is oppressive and real. Grief and mourning—an inevitable part of the ongoingness of life.

Sometimes life is thrust on us in a way that we have to mourn. We cannot postpone it. We cannot ignore it. It rips our hearts out, and we hurt and grieve.

A Choice

But Jesus speaks primarily of a spiritual mourning. A mourning that we choose. We could postpone it. We could ignore it. But we allow it to rip our hearts out. We choose to hurt and grieve. Bottom line, we choose God over self. After owning up to our own sin and to the grief we have brought to the heart of the compassionate creator God, we fall on our knees. After realizing we have broken his heart, our response is to bring him our hearts— vulnerable, contrite, humble. No other response makes sense. No other response brings healing. We choose to face the truth, and we are reconciled to our God.

Others might look at us and ask, "Why do you choose to mourn when you don't have to? It doesn't make any sense." To them God would say, *"Grieve, mourn and wail. Change your laughter to mourning and your joy to gloom"* (James 4:9).

We do not serve a sadistic God who enjoys our misery. We are not called to be masochists ourselves and to revel in our mournful response to this God. We are called to **life** by a pure and loving God who knows that only when we take on his selfless heart will we be able to know his boundless joy.

Spiritual mourning is an element of true repentance. It is the factor that initiates change. Paul puts it this way: *"Godly sorrow brings repentance that leads to salvation and leaves no regret..."* (2 Corinthians 7:10). It is not a matter of simply recognizing, admitting and cataloguing our sin. It is a matter of seeing ourselves in comparison to spiritual and moral perfection—not as a concept, but as a father who made us to be like him. We have hurt our Father, and when that realization touches our hearts, we want desperately to change from inside out and from top to bottom. That is repentance.

A Misunderstanding

In our response to our sin, we naturally tend toward one extreme or the other:

1. *Mournful mourning*—Woe-is-me, self-centered mourning that seeks to do penance. We find our identity by proving that our sin is worse than anyone else's. Then we talk about it and roll around in it and rub ourselves with it. We carefully shield ourselves from God's gracious offer of forgiveness. It's like leaving a gift-bearing friend on the front doorstep of our house in the pouring rain because we are just not worthy of accepting his/her gift. The focus is on our own unworthiness to the exclusion of God's grace. This is not the kind of mourning that brings about God's comfort.

2. *Matter-of-fact mourning*—This only qualifies as mourning because the mourner defines it as such. This response may be insightful and honest and even vulnerable—to a point. What is missing is the brokenness that gives birth to true spiritual mourning. The sacrifice that is pleasing to God is the one characterized by *"a broken and contrite heart"* (Psalm 51:17).

The cross is the center point within these two extremes. It is through our taking on that cross and the one who died on it for us that we can come to mourn our sins with proper perspective.

If we choose not to accept the guilt of our sin. . .one day we will. We cannot postpone it or ignore it forever. We cannot run enough, laugh enough, study enough, play enough to avoid the inevitable day of reckoning. The God who made everything also "made" this plan. His message to us is to quit hiding in our running, laughing, studying and playing long enough to listen to his offer of love and life. Those who listen and who respond will allow themselves to mourn. But rising from the ashes of that mourning, instantaneously will be joy, the purpose, the peace that God always meant for us to have.

A Softening

Having written most of this chapter earlier in the week, I sit here at my kitchen table thinking of an interchange I had with my husband tonight. During our discussion about a decision we and others need to make, I was brought face to face with a prideful, distrustful, unspiritual attitude—mine, not his. My family is asleep and I sit here alone thinking of what I have written about ignoring the sin, and I am fully aware of the futility of that approach. So I am tempted to rationalize it. It is a short jump to thinking how rotten I am (mournful mourning). Now I realize I am on my way to becoming a matter-of-fact mourner to ease the pain. No excuses. God's truth about mourning my sin is fresh on my mind and heart. I have written it, but will I live it?

That part of me on the inside that is holding on, "protecting" me from repentance is giving way. The dam of pride is cracking. As God's blessings flow in through the widening crack, I begin to remember why it is so blessed to mourn. I just want a soft heart, not a defensive rationale. Victory is assured when I know I am ready to share the softness with Tom—that is the test of humility. To lay down my excuses before God and not to pick them up again before man. Totally own it. Totally repent. Totally rejoice.

Are you postponing? Are you ignoring? Is your own reluctance to mourn keeping you from receiving the comfort God so much wants to give you?

SHEILA JONES
Concord, Mass.

FOR FURTHER STUDY:

Psalm 32
Psalm 51
Hosea 13:12-13,14:1-3
2 Corinthians 7:8-11

The Ease of Meekness

"Blessed are the meek, for they will inherit the earth" (Matthew 5:5).

T HE IDEA OF BEING MEEK IS NOT AN APPEALING ONE TO MOST people because they equate meekness with weakness. However, this is an absolute misconception! The Greek word for "meek" was used outside the New Testament to refer to a powerful stallion once it had been broken and had become teachable. He was in no way weak—just controllable. This third beatitude follows directly from the first two. Don't miss that. Once we have confronted our sin and experienced godly sorrow, we are no longer held captive by the pride that kept us from being teachable. We are free to receive correction and training. (The idea of being a good disciple shows up in some of the first things Jesus said!)

In the Bible meekness is associated with both humility and gentleness and is often translated with those words in the various English Bible versions. This meekness, humility or gentleness has no relation to a timid, retiring character but is a demonstration of deep conviction—the conviction that I need God and am totally open to *whatever* he wants to teach me through *whomever* he wants to use.

A look at some of the biblical characters who were said to be meek will help clear up any misconceptions we might have about this word. Moses was said to be very meek, in fact more meek than any man on the face of the earth (Numbers 12:3 KJV)! No one who is at all familiar with the Bible would ever accuse him of being weak! Jesus himself was said to be meek (2 Corinthians 10:1 NIV; Matthew 11:29 KJV). When you see him in the temple, consumed by righteous indignation, you would never think of the word weak!

At Ease

Meekness is strength under the control of God, and to those who exercise it, great promises are given. *"But the meek will inherit the land and enjoy great peace* "(Psalm 37:11). This type of peace carries the idea of being at ease before God and man. Meekness is built on great faith, for the meek person looks outside himself for the power to live. He is confident that because he is totally open to God, God will work in all things for his good.

To be meek is not to be afraid, but to be at ease—first of all, in the presence of God. Someone has said that worry and anxiety reduce us to practical atheists—we worry as if there were no God! The meek person has a powerful relationship with God. As the Psalmist put it, *"But I have stilled and quieted my soul; like a weaned child with its mother, like a weaned child is my soul within me"*(Psalm 131:2). Can't you just picture a child totally at ease and content in the presence of his mother? The meek person has that same relaxed calmness of spirit in the presence of his heavenly Father.

Second, the one who possesses meekness will be at ease with himself. He knows who he is and *whose* he is. In this quality he is like Jesus, the meek One whom we are to imitate. In John 13:3 we read that Jesus knew exactly what authority he had been given by God, and he knew where he had come from and where he was going. When we have surrendered to the purpose of God in our lives because we know our origin and destiny, we can relax, accepting who we are.

Third, the meek person will be at ease with others. He will feel neither inferior nor superior in their presence. No longer deceived by pride, he is free to learn from anybody. (No wonder he will inherit the earth!) At ease with God and himself, he now has nothing to prove and nothing to fear. He can now focus on serving other people in the fullest sense of the word because he has lost his sinful self-focus!

How to Grow It

Cultivating meekness is not simply a matter of going out and doing something. Since it is a character quality, it is not something that we do, but something we are. In Galatians 5:22 the quality of meekness (KJV—gentleness in the NIV) is listed as one of the fruits of the Holy Spirit. Therefore, he will have to produce this quality in us—with our cooperation. But just how do we cooperate?

Above all, realize how meekness follows poverty of spirit and godly sorrow. There is no shortcut to it. Try to jump over those first two beatitudes and you will never be meek. You fundamentally stay meek as you confront sin and work through it in a biblical fashion.

Beyond this there are some practicals that can make a difference:

(1) Study the nature of God in order to develop more reverence before him and more trust in him. Meekness is inseparably linked to both respect for God and faith in him.

(2) Study biblical passages on meekness and the related concepts of gentleness and humility and its opposite, pride. Hate the latter and pray for its total eradication from your life.

(3) Ask your closest relationships to help evaluate your humility and gentleness levels at the present time. Have them use the measurement of how much you are at ease in the presence of God, self and other people. Ask them how eager you seem to be to get input and help.

(4) Pray about what you see in the Bible and what you see in your own life in this area. Be specific and be hopeful. Expect God to change your heart and character through his Holy Spirit. Be patient but be persistent.

Now, how deep is your conviction? Do you want to be known as the meekest man or woman on the face of the earth? How earnestly will you seek this quality that Jesus says leads to inheriting the earth? Did you balk at any of the suggestions above about how to strive for meekness? Do you have some quiet reservations about meekness just not working in our world or particularly in your life?

Jesus was convicted about meekness. He preached it and he lived it, and now he says to you, "Follow me!"

GORDON FERGUSON
Danvers, Mass.

FOR FURTHER STUDY:

Galatians 5:22-23
Colossians 3:12
Titus 3:1-2
James 1:19-21, 3:13-18
1 Peter 3:13-16

Hunger

Hungry and Happy!

"Blessed are those who hunger and thirst for righteousness, for they will be filled" (Matthew 5:6).

BEING HUNGRY AND HAPPY AT THE SAME TIME DOES *NOT* SEEM correct. However, in the Kingdom, we *cannot* be truly happy (blessed) without first being hungry—hungry for God! Before and after this sermon Jesus performed many miracles and met many physical needs (Matthew 4:23-25). The people were happy and impressed with both his message and miracles. They were hungry and thirsty to have their physical needs met, but like most of us, the spiritual interest may not have been their primary focus. He wanted them to know that they could have lasting fulfillment only if they were longing to be filled with God.

Starving Without Him

Jesus was himself the Bread of Life (John 6:35), and the one who could give them living water (John 4:10). In John 4 after he offered the woman this living water, she was so happy that she went to share this new nourishment with all of her friends! Right after she left, Jesus told the disciples (who had just returned with food) that he had already *received* food. When they were puzzled by his response, he replied that his food was to do the will of God who had sent him and to accomplish his work. He was so happy about impacting this woman's life, and so caught up in doing God's will, that he literally lost his appetite!

Jesus is not talking here about someone who wants a nice little meal. He is describing an all-consuming *craving* for a relationship with him. It is seeking him with the urgency of starvation. Can you remember going without food or water for a prolonged period of time and how you could think of little else but satisfying the cravings of your body? Jesus is telling us that we need to live in this sort of state spiritually, not that we are to go around *unsatisfied*, but that we will stop at nothing to eat and drink of God!

The Psalmist understood well what Jesus meant: *"As the deer pants for streams of water, so my soul pants for you, O God. My soul thirsts for God, for the living God. When can I go and meet with God?"* (Psalm. 42:1-2). Just how *excited* are you about getting time to be with God every day? Do you make time? Are you looking for more time? Is your heart *yearning* to be with God?

Not only must we be hungry in our souls for an ever-deepening walk with God, but we must be hungry and thirsty for the Word of God. For a deeper conviction about loving the Word, read through the 119th Psalm. Over and over, the writer talks of loving God's law and meditating on it day and night. He is completely *delighted* with it, devoid of any sense of *duty* in reading it (for a quiet time), but *overjoyed* at the privilege of being able to commune with the expressed heart of his Creator!

As we feast on the Word of God, we will also hunger to please him, to obey him, to become more and more like him. This desire to please him will find a direct application in loving *others* as he does. Jesus hungered to serve others, to even give up his life for them. The *things of God* (Matthew 16:23) are all about serving and saving others for the glory of God. When our souls really do hunger for him, we will also hunger to bless the ones for whom Jesus died!

A Powerful Example

One of our greatest needs in growing spiritually is to keep an eternal perspective on our lives. We are not talking simply of being happy in the sense of enjoying our lives on this earth. Christianity is not another *self-help* approach to life, another *find yourself* philosophy. It is a religion teaching us how to *live* in order that we will know how to *die*. Christ is telling us how to live in *time* in order that we will live in *eternity*.

My own determination to hunger and thirst for righteousness was strengthened tremendously recently as a dear sister, Suzanne Atkins, faced death with an *amazing* hunger to see God. At age 32, with two small children, she discovered that she had a serious malignancy and would die in a matter of weeks. When I last saw her in San Diego just a few days before her death, I went for the purpose of encouraging her. However, *she* did most of the encouraging! As the pain of cancer wracked her body, her eyes were lit up with the thought of seeing the God for whom she had hungered and thirsted. Each morning when she awoke, she was *disappointed* that she had not yet gone to be with him. As we talked and laughed and prayed and wept, the real issues of righteousness came into clear perspective. The only way to hunger to be with God in the *next* life is to hunger to be with him *now* — every day! He is not a *part* of life — he *is* life itself.

Suzanne left behind a husband who is a disciple and two little boys who one day will be. And she left behind many friends, including me, who are more determined than ever to hunger and thirst for God. My prayer is that her example of dying with the joy of Jesus will help to create a thirst in you that will lead you to live and to die as she did. If *you* were to die *today*, what would others be able to honestly say about your hungering and thirsting for God and his righteousness? When we *live* out the beatitude of Matt. 5:6, then we can *die* with the beatitude of Revelation 14:13: "*'Blessed are the dead who die in the Lord from now on.' 'Yes,' says the Spirit, 'they will rest from their labor, for their deeds will follow them.'* "

THERESA FERGUSON
Danvers, Mass.

FOR FURTHER STUDY:

Psalm 18
Psalm 19
Psalm 42
Psalm 63
Philippians 3:7-14
Hebrews 5:11-14
1 Peter 2:1-3

Mercy

Just Like Our God

"Blessed are the merciful, for they will be shown mercy" (Matthew 5:7).

A FTER BEING FILLED WITH GOD'S RIGHTEOUSNESS, WHAT DOES JESUS expect of us? In the next beatitude he speaks about mercy. Mercy is so much a part of our Lord and our God.

We start by seeing our sin (Matthew 5:3) and mourning over it (v.4). Humbled by our need and grateful for the comfort God gives, we become open and teachable (v.5). Beyond that we now hunger to be filled with God himself (v.6). He responds, putting his Spirit and power into our lives. Once that happens, the most appropriate response? Treat others just like our God has treated us. That means show mercy.

There is much pain in our world. Starving children. Tortured prisoners. War-torn cities. Married couples living in hurt and mistrust. In all this, our God calls for mercy.

As Christians, we can listen to the cries for help and become numb. There is so much to do. We don't know where to start. So we just end up doing nothing. *"Because of the increase of wickedness, the love of most will grow cold, but he who stands firm to the end will be saved"* (Matthew 24:12-13). Has our love grown cold? Why do we feel so little mercy? Why don't we feel for others? When there is so much wickedness, we often think, "What can I do about it?" But if we are like our God, we know it will make a difference to show the world just what God has shown us: forgiveness, understanding and compassion.

Forgiveness

Getting into someone else's skin. Feeling what they feel. That's really what mercy is all about. What would it be like for us to be the other person in a given situation? Many times we are not merciful or forgiving because we get focused on ourselves and how we feel.

A few months ago, a sister really hurt me. I felt betrayed and used. It actually took me a whole month to forgive her from my heart! There were many things that I thought about during those weeks, but the center of my thoughts was "me." When I finally thought about the struggles and hardships that she was undergoing, I could feel compassion for her. Then all I wanted to do was to help her. Now our relationship is better than ever.

Probably there are many instances in which we can remember being hurt and having to forgive. Are those bitter feelings still there? Do you feel an ugly knot in your gut when you see that person? Actually, it doesn't matter how nicely we treat him or her if in our hearts we still have resentment or bitterness. These sins destroy our faith.

"Therefore, I tell you, whatever you ask for in prayer, believe that you have received it, and it will be yours. And when you stand praying, if you hold anything against anyone, forgive him, so that your Father in heaven may forgive you your sins" (Mark 11:24-25).

It says forgive **so that** your sins can be forgiven. *"Do not judge, and you will not be judged. Do not condemn and you will not be condemned. Forgive and you will be forgiven"* (Luke 6:37). We can always come up with what we think are valid reasons not to forgive. But Jesus is saying that there is no valid reason. Our lack of mercy blocks our relationship with God.

Let's think back to the times we have sinned against God. Remember the sins that are the most embarrassing and horrible. In fact, there might be some that you have never told anyone. Write them out and look at each one of those sins. Does it make you feel ugly to remember all of them?

"Once you were not a people, but now you are the people of God; once you had not received mercy, but now you have received mercy" (1 Peter 2:10). Just think, all those sins have been forgiven, erased and forgotten by God. Praise the Lord that we can have a new life in Christ! Then this new life calls us to forgive as we have been forgiven. God no longer holds your sins against you. Are you holding someone else's sins against him/her?

Understanding and Compassion

Mercy also comes in the form of understanding and compassion. For instance, *"As Jesus approached Jericho, a blind man was sitting by the roadside begging. When he heard the crowd going by, he asked what was happening. They told him, 'Jesus of Nazareth is passing by.' He called out, 'Jesus, Son of David, have mercy on me!'"* (Luke 18:35-43). Out of his compassion and understanding, Jesus gave him his sight. He had mercy on the blind beggar.

Although I do not have the gift to heal like Jesus, God has allowed me to minister to the hearts of those struggling with illness and physical handicaps. I have lupus, an illness that limits my activity, my lifestyle and my schedule. Before becoming sick, I didn't think much about people with chronic illnesses or physical disabilities. I would talk to such people and even feel sorry for them, but I could never feel *for* them deeply in an empathetic way. Because of my illness the last three years, I now have in my heart a feeling of mercy and care for those whose activities are limited by physical challenges. In fact, I can understand their struggles and help heal the pain in their hearts by sharing with them what I have learned and how I have overcome feeling sorry for myself. Having this illness has helped me become more like God—to see things more through his eyes. I am glad that God allowed me to be ill. I have learned a form of mercy that I would have never understood otherwise.

Truly, the merciful are blessed (superlatively happy) because they continue to receive mercy, even as they give it—especially as they give it. The greatest joy that we can have is our salvation in Christ. It comes totally from God's mercy. *"Therefore, I urge you, brothers, in view of God's mercy, to offer your bodies as living sacrifices, holy and pleasing to God—this is your spiritual act of worship"* (Romans 12:1). Let us worship God by showing the same mercy to others that he has shown to us.

ERICA KIM
Tokyo, Japan

FOR FURTHER STUDY:

1 Chronicles 21:13
Psalm 119:132
2 Corinthians 1:3-7
James 2:13
Jude 22-23

I Want to See God

"Blessed are the pure in heart, for they will see God" (Matthew 5:8).

HAVE YOU EVER STOOD AT THE BEACH AT NIGHT AND LOOKED ACROSS the water at the moon? Did you notice how the shaft of light always falls directly at your feet? Even if you were in a crowd of thousands, for you, the shaft of light would still fall at your feet. This is how it is for me when I read Jesus' words spoken to the multitudes on the mountain. He spoke to everyone who was there that day. And he spoke to everyone through the ages since that day. But, when I read it, he speaks directly to me. Today. He wants me to understand and accept this great truth: I must have a pure heart if I am to see God.

Jesus wants us to see God someday, just as he has seen him and known him and walked with him. That is the greatest blessing of all—to see God. Certainly, Jesus wants us to see God at work in our lives, but in this context, he wants us to *see* God. Ultimately— to be able to stand in the presence of our creator on the final day.

Guarding Against Heart Disease

What does it mean to keep our hearts pure? To be undivided in our devotion to God. From the time we are raised in Christ at baptism, we set our hearts on things above (Colossians 3:1). From that very moment, Satan launches an attack on our hearts. He has been dethroned and he wants to work his disease of deceit right back into our hearts. So we must learn how to battle Satan's heart attacks.

In recent years people have become increasingly aware of their physical heart conditions. They learn the symptoms of heart disease; they lower their cholesterol intake, and they master the stair master. Why do they make such effort? They desire a disease free heart. They consider it worth their time and effort to be informed, to diet and to exercise because they *want to*. The heart is the "want to" muscle; it is the "muscle of desire." When we really want something, we go after it with all of our heart. Spiritually, we must want to know about the things that can cause heart disease. For the physical heart, often the cause is too much cholesterol. Spiritually speaking, worry and the guilt of sin are the cholesterol that clogs our hearts. (See Matthew 6:24 and Mark 7:20-23.)

I have learned a lot about heart disease from Luke 7:36-50 when Simon said to himself, *"If this man were a prophet..."* Simon had quiet reservations about Jesus. He had doubts, but he did not say what he thought. Simon let his silence and pride so damage his heart that he had no gratitude, no eagerness to serve and no compassion or forgiveness.

I went through a time in my own life when I kept my mouth shut and tried to "be a good disciple." Two weeks after the birth of our first child, my mother died. No one had ever accepted me like my mother had. No one had ever loved me in the pure way that she had. After her death, I withdrew my heart and refused to give it out again. I was afraid to be vulnerable and open with others. Instead of being thankful that I had been privileged to know such love, I despaired that I would never know it again. Because of holding back my heart, I began to keep my quiet reservations, my fears and my anger to myself also. I slowly became critical and bitter with my husband, church leaders and even the lost. It was a miserable time for me. I lost my convictions. The cholesterol of guilt and worry had clogged my burdened heart. God used this time to show me how I must always strive to keep a pure heart.

A Healthy Heart

How can we get a pure heart? Physically of course the key is proper diet and adequate exercise of the heart muscle. It is the same spiritually. What is your spiritual diet? Are you dependent on his word? Too often as women we want to talk and get all of our feelings out and be counseled when what we really need to do is sit down and read the Bible. The Word is what purifies us. It discerns the thoughts and attitudes of our hearts. It will diagnose us and sanctify us. In Psalm 119:9 David says we can keep our hearts pure by *"living according to [God's] word."* David did more than snack on the Scriptures, he made sure they were his steady diet.

In his desire to maintain a pure heart, David says, *"I will set before my eyes no vile thing"* (Psalm 10:13). We need to cut unhealthy food out of our spiritual diets. What do you read? What do you watch or listen to? Will it clog up your heart spiritually, or will it keep it pumping steadily?

Secondly, we need to exercise our heart in order to make it strong. How do we do this? Be honest. Be vulnerable. Push through and say what you think even when it is difficult. Serve when it is not convenient. Forgive when you have been treated unfairly. Obedience to the truth purifies our hearts (1 Peter 1:22). A strong heart is a heart that is always being put to the test for God. God has tested our hearts by moving us to lead ministries in Bangkok, Manila, and California within a four-year-span. We had to exercise our hearts by learning to give freely and quickly to many different types of people.

What has kept me faithful during the difficult times—the lonely years of being a single woman, the hurt of losing both of my parents, the unsettling times of seeing my failures in my marriage, the disappointments of miscarrying our first baby at four months, the challenging time of having a baby at 40 in Bangkok, the sad moments of knowing that some whom I have trusted have left God, and the uncertainty of the four weeks when I sat by my 2-year-old daughter's bed in a Manila hospital? It has been my intense desire to see God. In those times my motivation came from remembering Jesus' words like the shaft of moonlight at my feet, *"Blessed are the pure in heart, for they will see God."*

EMILY BRINGARDNER
Los Angeles, Calif.

FOR FURTHER STUDY:

Psalm 51:10
Psalm119:1-16
Titus 1:15, 2:11-14
1 John 1:7-9, 3:1-3

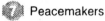

Peace in Our Time

"Blessed are the peacemakers, for they will be called sons of God"
(Matthew 5:9).

WAR. DIVORCE. HATE CRIMES. RIOTS. RACISM. ETHNIC CLEANSING.
Custody battles. Hostile takeovers. Domestic violence.
The world knows little of peace. But God wages peace.
The heart of God is to be at peace with man. He created us in
order to have relationship with us. Jesus did say, *"Do not suppose
that I have come to bring peace to the earth. I did not come to bring
peace, but a sword"* (Matthew 10:34). Yet he also said, *"Peace I
leave with you; my peace I give you"* (John 14:27). Is this
contradictory? Not when we understand that in order for true peace
to occur, we must resolve the wars in our hearts and in the hearts
of those around us. You can't understand peace until you dare to
face the conflicts and wars in your life. You can't have peace until
you take Jesus' sword into your life. Peace is not conflict
avoidance, it is resolution after a spiritual war.

Making Peace with God

Being a peacemaker begins with being at peace with our
maker. Only those who know God can make peace that endures.
Paul reminds us, *"Once you were alienated from God and were
enemies in your minds because of your evil behavior"* (Colossians
1:21). We were separated from him and were at war with him. But
now the war is over. And we need to live like it is over. Jesus' blood
and his stubborn stand against sin brought us peace with God. After
humbling our hearts and mourning over our sins before him, we are
now God's children and he is our Father. We are in a family—a real
family.

But keeping peace with God is an ongoing process. Our lives
must be continually cleansed from the sin that wages war with God.
Guards must be posted at the doors of our hearts to keep out the

enemies of peace. Right now how is the level of peace in your life? Have worries slipped past your watchman to rob you of your trust in him? Are there any secrets that make you hide in darkness again? Is there any unresolved or unconfessed sin that still wars within your heart? If so, you are missing out on the peace God so much wants you to have.

Making Peace with Others

But once we are one with God, contrary to the lives of many religious people, the story of peace is not over. As we maintain our peace with God, his heart becomes our own, and we are propelled out into our world to wage peace just as he does.

Jesus is our example. With courage and honesty he destroyed the barriers that could have separated him from people. Openly expressing his thoughts and feelings to others, he pulled down walls of superficiality and distrust. He expressed his fears (Matthew 26:36-46), his disappointment (Matthew 11:14-17), his joy (Luke 10:18-22), his anger and frustration (Matthew 23). He expressed that which was on his heart even though it might have caused conflicts. Developing friendships with different people, he showed others how to end discrimination and prejudice. Whether Jew or Samaritan, man or woman, rich or poor, healthy or sick, Pharisee or prostitute, ruler or tax collector, they were all people he wanted in his family. He wanted people to be **totally** united, regardless of the differences.

As a disciple, making peace with others is a challenge. It takes honesty and vulnerability—traits that we do not naturally have. Jesus pulled down all walls, but our pride, distrust and anger build walls between us and other disciples. Are there any hidden attitudes or "funny feelings" toward others? Any discrimination? Any unresolved issues in your marriage or close relationships? If you want real peace, don't avoid conflict. Follow the example of the Prince of Peace. Do whatever is required to *"settle matters quickly"* and restore peace.

Helping Others to Make Peace

Our highest calling as peacemakers is to *help* others make peace with God. Paul tells us to have our feet *"fitted with the readiness that comes from the gospel of peace"* (Ephesians 6:15).

Because of the peace with God that Jesus has brought to our lives, we are ready to have feet that *"bring good news"* and *"proclaim peace"* to others (Isaiah 52:7). Jesus never compromised his mission or his purpose. Whether he was rested or tired, encouraged or discouraged, praised or despised, he was always ready to help others make peace with God. Jesus, **the** peacemaker shed his blood so we could have peace. And he calls us to die to ourselves so others can be made right with God.

We must be determined to carry out the mission assigned us in Matthew 28—bringing peace to the world. Not a superficial "world peace," but true peace in the heart of each man and each woman. To accomplish this mission Jesus kept his standards high, even in the face of criticism, persecution and doubt. We can do no less. We must be certain to call each man to God's standards for reconciliation with him. We should never compromise to make it easier for people to respond.

Recently, I studied the Bible with a woman who was eager to become a Christian but slow to open up her life to discipling and to resolve past relationships. She was eager for forgiveness, but not for repentance. As we studied with her, I stayed firm on God's standard of what it means to be a disciple of Jesus. At times I felt we were waging a war against each other, but I kept in mind that God and I were waging war against Satan for this woman's soul. Then came the distinct time, as we studied sin, that she truly saw her need for peace with God and accepted his standard—total surrender. She is now a faithful disciple—and at peace.

Being a peacemaker will cost us. Time. Energy. Comfort. But wars that lead to lasting peace are worth fighting.

Specifically, how can you wage peace in your world today?

LYNNE GREEN
Hong Kong

FOR FURTHER STUDY:

John 14:27
Romans 5:1-5
Galatians 5:19-26
Ephesians 2:14-18
1 Timothy 2:3-6

Pain and Gain

"Blessed are those who are persecuted because of righteousness, for theirs is the kingdom of heaven. Blessed are you when people insult you, persecute you and falsely say all kinds of evil against you because of me. Rejoice and be glad, because great is your reward in heaven, for in the same way they persecuted the prophets who were before you" (Matthew 5:10-12).

T HOSE WHO HAVE DECIDED TO FOLLOW JESUS CHRIST ARE ALL being persecuted, and it is hard to be glad about it. Every day that we reach for what is right, we grasp, often unexpectedly and often unwittingly, the unforgiving thorns of persecution:

• A Boston teen declines the chance to follow the senseless crowd and is considered by his peer group to be "out-of-it"—a reject.
• A Paris woman offers problem-solving counsel to another only to find it provokes an angry, resentful response.
• A Tokyo Christian employee is openly pressured by boss and colleagues to forsake church in order to work overtime and prove "company loyalty."
• A Hong Kong new convert returns home each evening to be verbally blasted by his parents.
• A Bombay disciple is threatened, beaten and tortured by her own family.

At War

We do not ask to be persecuted; we certainly do not want to be persecuted, and most of us cannot imagine, really, the more severe and physical persecutions happening to us or our family. But persecutions must come and will come to every single person who tries to live a godly life (2 Timothy 3:12). The reason why they must come is that we are at war. We may pretend that life is not war. We may wish to see life as a party, or as a contest, or a nice story of growth and gentle aging, but the hard and unyielding truth is that life is a spiritual war, even for those who are not aware of spiritual things. Thus Jesus says, without apology, *"I did not come to bring peace, but a sword"* (Matthew 10:34). He knew that life means war.

Knowing that life means war will not make us glad to be persecuted, but it will make us ready—ready for trouble, difficulty, hardship, persecution. Only in the role of warrior, then, can we begin to understand why Jesus dares to say, *"Blessed are those who are persecuted."* It is like saying, "Blessed are the fighters, the people of courage who choose to fight Satan's opposition rather than run." And here Jesus shows us how, in the thick of that fight, to find peace.

Blessings

The blessings of persecution are at least three. In Matthew 5:10 Jesus declares Blessing Number One to be that of the Kingdom of heaven itself: *"for theirs is the kingdom of heaven."* This really sounds like persecution guarantees my entrance into heaven. But even non-Christians are persecuted for righteousness at times, and we know they are **not** on their way to heaven. I see this blessing in the same context as 1 Peter 1:6-7: *"In this you greatly rejoice, though now for a little while you may have had to suffer grief in all kinds of trials. These have come so that your faith—of greater worth than gold, which perished even though refined by fire—may be proved genuine...."* Opposition, difficulty, persecution all test my faith, refining it in fire so that it may be proved genuine. And genuine faith must be, by definition, all-weather faith! Persecution separates fair-weather pretenders from real disciples of Christ.

The Second Blessing is similar to the first: *"great is your reward in heaven."* It is a promise ignored by most disciples. In our efforts to remain grateful and broken before the Lord, we are often insensitive to the very positive fact that God greatly desires to reward us. In the name of grace, we focus on the fact that our Father keeps no record of wrongs, but forget that he is keeping a record of rights! *"He will **not** forget your work and the love you have shown him"* (Hebrews 6:10).

The greatness of the reward is not lost for the pure in heart. On one occasion my son Stephen, just four-years-old, showed me how real it should be. Walking on one of Hong Kong's narrow sidewalks with double decker busses intermittently whizzing by, I told him to stay close and watch out for cars. He answered with a triumphant, "I don't care!" As I readied myself to correct his "rebellion," he went on: "I don't care, because, well, if a car hits me. . .I'll just go right on to heaven to live with God, Dad." I still needed to ensure his safety, but heaven was real to him and made him feel secure with

disasters whizzing by in his little life. Is it that real to you?
"The prophets who were before you" (v.12) bring the Third
Blessing. Persecution and suffering mean pain, but they also mean
glory. The glory comes in realizing we walk in the company of the
glorious, in knowing we are doing and enduring exactly the same
things done and endured by those we hold in awe. The *"great cloud
of witnesses"* in Hebrews 12—prophets and martyrs of the Old
Testament—shows me the way and inspires my perseverance. As I
fix my eyes on Jesus, who scorned the shame of his persecution, my
courage is more than inspired. My pain is real, but his was far worse!

Nothing in Comparison

Disciples in our generation have endured beatings, torture,
kidnapping, riots, hostile police and officials, and the perils of
catacomb Christianity. My own troubles seem like less than nothing
when I remember my brothers and sisters in Mainland China. As of
this writing, disciples in China must meet, study their Bibles, and
pray in secret. They evangelize at great risk. They rarely have Bible
discussions for non-Christians because of the danger of being turned
in by a stranger. They cannot allow unbelievers to attend Sunday
services, and so those non-Christians studying the Bible never get
to see the body of Christ until after baptism. In spite of these
limitations, they grow quickly, devoting themselves to the Word, to
a challenging fellowship, and to family. Each new disciple leads
another study with a non-Christian friend. They don't complain
about what they don't have, but rejoice in the salvation they do have.

Peter writes: *"Stand firm in the faith, because you know that
your brothers throughout the world are undergoing the same kind
of sufferings"* (1 Peter 5:9). Or worse, much worse.

God saved each of us from an empty way of life; he never
promised an easy one. Count it as a great, great blessing to suffer
for the Name.

SCOTT GREEN
Hong Kong

FOR FURTHER STUDY:

John 15:18-25
1 Peter 4
Revelation 2-3

Taste the Difference

"You are the salt of the earth. But if salt loses its saltiness, how can it be made salty again? It is no longer good for anything except to be thrown out and trampled by men" (Matthew 5:13).

I N ANY SITUATION IT IS IMPORTANT TO UNDERSTAND YOUR IDENTITY and your role. Jesus frequently told his disciples who they were and what they should be as spiritual people in an unspiritual world. We are to be godly men and women among godless men and women and disciples of Jesus among those who are not his disciples. Jesus' point here is:

> You are different!
> You need to be different!
> You are happier when you are different!

To show us how to be distinctive Jesus used many analogies and metaphors. One of his clearest is that of salt. Commonly known and used, salt was easily understood as a metaphor of life in the Kingdom of God. Salt was used as an antiseptic to cleanse and purify. It was used in foods to preserve and to "bring the best out" in terms of taste and quality. Salt was used in ratifying covenants under Old Testament law because of its role as a preservative and producer of lasting effect. God required that it be put in animal sacrifices and grain offerings signifying a lasting covenant with God and making them pleasing to him. (Leviticus 2:13, Ezra 6:9)

Conspicuous Character

It was with this background of Old Testament significance that Jesus used salt to describe the spiritual identity of his disciples. He calls us to be the preservers of righteousness in the midst of godless lifestyles. To be the "conspicuous character that brings out the best" in human nature in contrast to so much that shows man's worst.

In the Beatitudes Jesus gives the vital ingredients for spiritual salt. It seems to me they can be put in two categories that every disciple must possess! In verses 3-9 Jesus describes the conspicuous ingredients of a salty character. We must be different from the inside out. We are the salt of the earth by what we are at the heart and conviction level. Jesus calls us to be poor in spirit not proud and to cry over our sin and the sin of the world instead of being hardened to it. He calls us to be eager and teachable, even hungry for righteousness. Such a hunger will result in mercy and purity of heart. These are the traits God wants preserved and promoted in our lives. Each disciple must ask, "Do I have a conspicuous character that God can point the world to and say, 'Be like him or her on the inside'?" Our oldest daughter was in a state pageant for teens several years ago. Parents of each contestant were asked to write an essay on why their daughter should represent the teen spirit desired in our state. With tears, I read the winning letter about the love, service, joy, conviction and other salty qualities she possessed as a disciple. She was picked as "Miss Teen Spirit" because Jesus had produced a conspicuous charactor that was salt of the earth in quality. Does your character win the world's respect and admiration because of its "salty" flavor?

Prophetic Posture

Disciples of Jesus are salty not only because of a changed character but also a prophetic posture. Matthew 5:9-12 indicates that what we say and what is said about us are also necessary ingredients to qualify as salt of the earth. Disciples, like the prophets of old, must stand up and speak out for God regardless of the reaction it brings from the world! They call people to make peace with God on his terms.

Bold and insistent voices can be heard in our time for "no fault" divorce, gay rights, abortion rights, free sex, recreational drugs and many other ungodly positions. We must be the salt of the earth—voices that expose and challenge these views from the word of God. From the youngest teen disciple to the oldest married or single disciple, we must take a prophetic posture that is unashamed of Jesus and his words. I remember speaking to a college sociology class on Christian marriage. A rowdy reaction ensued after I laid out biblical expectations of purity, morality, leadership and submission. Some walked away angry, but two of these class members began to study the Bible and eventually were baptized as disciples. Paul wrote, *"Let your conversation be seasoned with salt"*(Colossians 4:6). This includes a prophetic posture that speaks the truth in love without hesitation or lack of conviction.

In three different places Jesus is recorded as saying salt is good, but if it loses its flavor it becomes good for nothing. The conspicuous character must keep developing, for none of us are yet like Jesus. He said it himself: We must hunger and thirst for even more righteousness. Our prophetic posture must be maintained and further developed as part of our effort to "win as many as possible" from the deceptions of the world. We cannot be powerful people who penetrate and influence our world if we no longer have convictions about changing and growing ourselves. A disciple who *once* hungered for righteousness is a tragic sight. He is the salt that has lost its saltiness and is good for nothing. "Once salt, always salt" is not found in your Bible. Jesus is saying you can be salt and make a difference in the lives of others and then lose even your own salvation by turning back to the world or becoming half-hearted in your discipleship. He who has ears, let him hear!

Disciple, Jesus wants you to understand who you are and what a difference you can make in the lives of those around you. But are you different? Are you distinct? Are you good for nothing or good for everybody as the salt of the earth?

WYNDHAM SHAW
Burlington, Mass.

FOR FURTHER STUDY:

Numbers 18:17-19
2 Chronicles 13:4-7
Colossians 4:2-6
Titus 2:3-10
1 Peter 2:11-12

Let It Shine

"You are the light of the world. A city on a hill cannot be hidden. Neither do people light a lamp and put it under a bowl. Instead they put it on its stand, and it gives light to everyone in the house. In the same way, let your light shine before men, that they may see your good deeds and praise your Father in heaven" (Matthew 5:14-16).

D O YOU KNOW PEOPLE WHO SIMPLY CANNOT HIDE WHAT THEY ARE thinking? Their faces always tell the truth. Moses was that type of person. When he came down from Mount Sinai with the two tablets in his hands, he did not know that his face was radiant. His face showed clearly that he had been in the presence of Almighty God (Exodus 34:29).

Throughout time God's presence in a person's life has produced a great radiance. Jesus, embodying the full presence of God, states, *"I am the light of the world. Whoever follows me will never walk in darkness, but will have the light of life"* (John 8:12).

It is one thing to be inspired by Moses' great radiance and to be awed by Jesus as the light of the world, but we too must embrace our calling. Jesus said to ordinary men and women: *"You are the light of the world."* Every disciple, without exception, who lives out the beatitudes at the beginning of this sermon will powerfully shine God's light into the world. They will not just cheer up a place; they will do nothing less than reveal to others the nature of God and the meaning of life!

Light Gives Direction

Without light we do not know where to walk. We do not know when to turn or how to reach our destination. We become disoriented because there is nothing to point us on our way. God has throughout time provided light for direction. When the Israelites left Egypt heading for the promised land, God went before them at night in a pillar of fire to show them where to go.

As the wise men searched for the Savior of the world, they knew the direction to go because God sent them starlight. Likewise, in a dark world where people are *"helpless and harassed, like sheep without a shepherd,"* your life can give direction. Your humility, your hunger for truth, your mercy can be a star for others to follow. Your willingness to get help and change in some area of your life can provide others a direction most do not have.

Your purity of heart and concern for integrity can shake up the business world. Your faith and joy in the face of trials can show others that with God there is a way out of anything. This world is in desperate need of direction and you, disciples, are the light of the world.

Light Drives Satan Away

"God is light; in him there is no darkness at all" (1 John 1:5). Satan hates for the light to be on. He cannot be where there is light. When the light comes on, sin is exposed. Your life can contrast and expose sin. You can stand up with conviction for the teachings of Jesus when they are not popular. You can humble yourself and take ownership when you have done wrong. In either case light comes on and sin is exposed for what it is. Certainly, the light you give will bring reaction from others. Some will run and others will try to put it out. Thankfully, still others will be drawn to it and will pursue new direction in their lives. It is for them that God has put you there.

"This is the verdict: Light has come into the world, but men loved darkness instead of light because their deeds were evil. Everyone who does evil hates the light, and will not come into the light for fear that his deeds will be exposed. But whoever lives by the truth comes into the light, so that it may be seen plainly that what he has done has been done through God" (John 3:19-21). Light takes away Satan's power. As Samson was powerless without his hair, Satan is powerless without darkness. There are things in my life I've been afraid of or embarrassed about. Once I talked about them, they were in the light. Satan then no longer had control of my fear. The more we open ourselves up to God's light, the more his light shines through us to expose the darkness. You are the light of the world!

Light Gives Life

Without light all of creation would die. Many people today have more of an existence than a life, carrying the burden of sin and hopelessness on their shoulders. David describes this condition caused by separation from God in Psalm 38:10, *"My heart pounds, my strength fails me; even the light has gone from my eyes."* But you can show others what it is like to have light in your eyes. When you have surrendered to God's will and are knowing the joy of his work in your life, others will see a sparkle. Some of us aren't shining very brightly because we are trying to be disciples without surrendering. Others cannot see in us how death produces life (and power and joy) because we aren't dying. The only way to turn the light of Christ on is to die to self. There is nothing more useless and frustrating than a burned out light bulb. It is counted on, yet unavailable. Is your light counted on, yet unavailable, or is it a beacon for the lost world?

Let it Shine!

"You are the light of the world. . . .Let it shine," said Jesus. "Don't put it under a bowl. Let it shine!" And so today wherever you will be, let it shine! Someone out there needs for you to let it shine. Don't put it under a bowl of timidity or insecurity. Let it shine! Don't put it under a bowl of busyness and rushing. Let it shine! Don't put it under a bowl of selfishness. Let it shine! Are you facing some stiff challenge? All the more reason to let it shine! Don't let Satan blow it out. Start in your own household. Be humble and meek and let it shine. Go out in the world and be merciful and compassionate and let it shine. Tell others about this powerful faith, and rejoice even if they reject you and let it shine!

Yes, you *are* the light of the world! Let it shine!

JEANIE SHAW
Burlington, Mass.

FOR FURTHER STUDY:

Isaiah 53:10-11
John 1:1-9
Romans 13:11-14
2 Corinthians 4:5-6
Ephesians 5:3-14
1 John 1:1-10

Part 2

Heart

 Righteousness

Taking It to a New Level

"For I tell you that unless your righteousness surpasses that of the Pharisees and the teachers of the law, you will certainly not enter the kingdom of heaven" (Matthew 5:20).

J ERUSALEM, 27 AD. IMAGINE THE SCENE: NARROW STREETS crammed tight with Jews and foreigners, tax collectors, detachments of Roman soldiers, merchants and vendors of every possible ware, children, livestock, laborers and craftsmen, the sick. The aromas of Middle Eastern food, blended with smoke from the Temple, human sweat, animal smells. And seemingly everywhere, those respected men: the priests, Sadducees and Pharisees.

Majoring in Minors

Pharisee—the very word has strong associations. Pharisees: those strict observers of the Law, 6,000 of them in Judea but especially in the great city of Jerusalem. Not all were hypocrites, but so few had pure motives that Jesus later will strongly challenge them all as one group (Matthew 23). Walking around in their flowing robes, offering prayers in unnaturally holy voices on the street corners, advertising their benevolence with pride, pomp and fanfare. They looked down on the common people who took few pains to observe the many Pharisaic traditions accumulated through the centuries.

Majoring in the minutiae of the law, yet forgetting the heart and soul behind it. Legalistic, lackluster, seldom loving. Dry, drab, dull, dusty! No wonder the common man was turned off to religion! No wonder Jesus' energy, authority, love and zeal stood out in such stark contrast!

But is it any different today? The average man or woman forms a concept of "religion" based on what is portrayed by the religious "powers that be." Boring clergymen in odd clothes and tinny, holy voices, preaching burdensome do's and don't's, unrelatable sermons backed up by unrelatable lives. Legalism, regulations, religion—we have enough of that in our world!

What people need and inwardly want is a relationship with God, not a man-made religion. So what did he have to say, this new rabbi, Jesus? He came. And he preached. His aim: to teach the real meaning of righteousness, which is far more profound than the common, skin-deep religiosity of the Pharisees. This crucial section of the Sermon on the Mount is essential for understanding the entire sermon.

Many, if not most, Christians today are confused by this preface and the "You have heard it said" comments that follow. But if we don't figure it out, we may just find ourselves slowly slipping into the spiritual hardening of Pharisaism.

Mortals Can Go to Heaven!

Listen to Jesus: *"Unless your righteousness exceeds the righteousness of the scribes and Pharisees, you will never enter the kingdom of heaven."* Be challenged—religiosity will not impress God. Not yours, not anybody's. But be encouraged—a heart for God and a heart for people will be richly rewarded. It is possible for mortals to go to heaven! But we'll have to have very different hearts from those "clergymen" of Jesus' day. These "experts" in the law were adept at watering down or avoiding outright the plain meaning of God's word, cleverly explaining it away in a tangle of exceptions, provisos, qualifiers and speculation. Their intent was to make themselves look good, not to please God and love their neighbors whatever the costs.

A righteousness that surpasses that of the Pharisees doesn't mean perfection unless, perhaps, it refers to the righteousness of later NT passages that mean a perfect moral standing before God through Christ. Much more likely here, it refers to the usual OT definition of righteousness (upright dealings with others).

This really is good news! A perfect religion is not the basis of our salvation. Jesus isn't saying if you break any commandment at all you won't go to heaven. In fact, he implies (earlier in v. 19) that you could break a command or even teach others to disregard a command and still make it to heaven—though not without some loss, as *"least in the kingdom of heaven"* makes clear. Besides, some commandments (especially those Jesus doesn't take up in the Sermon on the Mount) are more important than others (Matthew 23:23). So don't be afraid: Your salvation depends not on your perfection, but on his. This passage is not a call to be ultra-righteous. It's a call to be righteous—to have the kind of heart Jesus began this sermon with in the Beatitudes—something about which many religious people know far too little.

Any Pharisee in You?

Do you struggle with Pharisaism? Careful now! Ever do things for show (Matthew 6)—to be "seen by men" (fellow Christians, church leaders, roommates, spouse, children, anyone)? If no one were watching would you bother to pray, to sing out, to contribute? Do people say you're a people-pleaser (Galatians 1:10)? Maybe you're finding your way around commands instead of just obeying them. Perhaps you make deals with yourself: "Today I don't need to share my faith because I studied my Bible extra long this morning." What good lawyers we can be! The religious world is full of lawyers. They aren't fulfilled, though, and they're certainly not happy. Joy comes when we trust and obey. There's no other way!

We all have our nice little system. But are we trying to be saved by it? Often I've caught myself drifting into this mindset. Thinking that consistent discipline, getting up on time, giving 10%, daily prayer, reading, evangelism and my appointment book will save me. The fact is, these things consistently practiced are extremely helpful for growing as a Christian, but they don't save us! And when we create rules (whether or not they have a biblical motivation) and insist that not to follow them is sin, we've stepped over the line. God's commands are commands, advice is advice.

Finally, how's our knowledge of the Bible, including the Old Testament? (As the Hebrew writer said, it's *"living and active."*) Are we comfortable with it, familiar with it, handy with it? Do we appreciate its majesty, power, accuracy and penetrating insight into our hearts? Or are we more steeped in our own traditions, methodology and preconceived notions about the truth? For unless our righteousness surpasses...

DOUGLAS JACOBY
Washington, D.C.

FOR FURTHER STUDY:

Leviticus 19:1-37
Deuteronomy 30:11-20
Matthew 15:1-20
Matthew 23:1-32
Romans 10:1-8

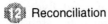 Reconciliation

Rapid Resolution

"You have heard that it was said to the people long ago, 'Do not murder, and anyone who murders will be subject to judgment.' But I tell you that anyone who is angry with his brother will be subject to judgment.... Therefore, if you are offering your gift at the altar and there remember that your brother has something against you, leave your gift there in front of the altar. First go and be reconciled to your brother; then come and offer your gift. Settle matters quickly...." (Matthew 5:21-25).

ARE YOU A CONFLICT AVOIDER? "WELL... UM... SORT OF, I guess..."Is that your response? Your hesitancy spells out the answer very clearly: Y-E-S! We spend all our life avoiding conflict, covering things up, running away from unpleasant situations. Now we become Christians, and God expects us to be direct, to actually go to the other person, even when we are not the ones with the problem. To grab the bull by the horns if we only suspect he or she has something against us. Some attitude, some grudge, some thought less than worthy of our Lord. What an adjustment that was for me! What a new way of thinking and relating to other people!

A New Teaching?

Was this a new teaching coming from Jesus? Was he totally changing the Old Testament message? Often today we think of the Old Testament as the list of do's and don't's—the "law" given by a harsh, punitive God just waiting for us to break it. But really that's a misunderstanding. The Old Testament is fully consistent with the New Testament—we just aren't as familiar with it. The issue between God and man is the heart! Actually, Matthew 5:21-26 has its Old Testament counterpart in Leviticus 19, *"Do not go about spreading slander among your people. Do not do anything that endangers your neighbor's life. I am the Lord. Do not hate your brother in your heart. Rebuke your neighbor frankly so that you will not share in his guilt. Do not seek revenge or bear a grudge against one of your people, but love your neighbor as yourself. I am the Lord"* (Leviticus 19:16-18).

God does look at the heart, and he always has. The heart isn't something he just started noticing in the first century! The Bible—the whole Bible—reveals the character of God. And the Bible says we should love our neighbor not just out of fear of punishment or even because it's the correct thing to do, but because God is God, and any other behavior is inconsistent with his character (vv.16, 18).

Responsibility in Relationships

Jesus basically tells us that we are responsible to be righteous in every relationship. He refers to using the word, "raca," which was an Aramaic term of contempt. So, what was the difference between raca and fool? Apparently the Sanhedrin had a rule about the R-word. Jesus says it's more than just one word, more than even a certain list of forbidden words. It's about the thoughts and attitudes of our hearts. If hate is in the heart, we're condemning ourselves.

We must deal with conflict instead of pretending it's not there. We don't have altars today, but we still worship. Jesus didn't say we're not allowed to worship if we have an enemy somewhere. Any true follower of the Kingdom will have enemies, as Jesus assured us in Matthew 5:11-12. And he tells us all about how to deal with enemies at the end of Matthew 5. But this section is about our brothers and sisters. And whether or not it's our problem, we have the responsibility to seek the person out, speak frankly, and make every effort to build unity. Failing to resolve things with a sister or brother will erode our relationship with God. Our worship is not pleasing to God. So if this is your situation, "leave your gift"—that is, sort things out as soon as possible!

We need to resolve things quickly, before the sun goes down. Otherwise rumors spread, or we land ourselves in an impossible situation. Waiting only makes things worse. Consider Jesus' example of the lawsuit. The type of illustration Jesus chose emphasizes the eternal importance of men and women who sort things out quickly! Is that your character?

Take the Teaching Home

Are there any uncomfortable situations in your life right now? Don't wait for the other person to come to you. Seek out the one you think has an attitude against you. Don't think, "It's his responsibility. It's his problem, not mine!" Because if you don't work things out, it will become your problem. Matthew 18 even teaches us that if all efforts to resolve things are unsuccessful, it needs to become a public (or "family") affair. Have you ever pushed something that far, been that determined to build unity? Paul said, *"Make every effort to keep the unity of the Spirit. . ."* (Ephesians 4:3).

Are you a conflict avoider? Ask others to tell you what they see in your character; pray to God for divine power not to slip back; but most important, make a decision today to change. If you do, you can change quickly. Don't automatically assume it is the other person's fault. There may be something in your own heart you had not noticed. Hatred is like murder. It rejoices in the downfall of the person you have a problem with. Through the sharpness of the tongue it assassinates his or her character. Do you have attitudes toward someone else? Should someone else be seeking you out because of your attitudes?

Get motivated. Take the initiative. Don't wait for someone else to tell you that you need to sort things out. People who act only when confronted are often hypersensitive. Are you touchy? Are you a "wheelbarrow Christian"—one who always has to be pushed and is easily upset? Jesus does not allow us the easy way out. Love is tough. Love speaks the truth (Ephesians 4:25).

Last of all, remember that relationships with others mirror our true relationship with God. And we'll never be close to the God of truth if we're afraid to speak the truth to our fellow man.

VICKI JACOBY
Washington, D.C.

FOR FURTHER STUDY:

Leviticus 19:1-37
Matthew 18:15-20
Galatians 1:10
Ephesians 4:20-32
Colossians 1:28-2:2, 3:7-14
Titus 3:1-5
James 4:11
1 Peter 2:1

Radical Righteousness

"You have heard that it was said, 'Do not commit adultery.' But I tell you that anyone who looks at a woman lustfully has already committed adultery with her in his heart. If your right eye causes you to sin, gouge it out and throw it away. It is better for you to lose one part of your body than for your whole body to be thrown into hell. And if your right hand causes you to sin, cut it off and throw it away. It is better for you to lose one part of your body than for your whole body to go into hell" (Matthew 5:27-30).

SOME OF US WHO THINK MORE ANALYTICALLY WORK BEST WITH RULES and checklists. We are the ones who blend in well with the Pharisees: "Moses said not to commit adultery; well, I'm not guilty of that so I can check off another item on my *Get to Heaven* 'To Do' *List.*" I'm tempted to reduce Christianity to a list of a couple of pages of rules to examine myself by:

Baptized	X Yes	___No
Daily Quiet Time	X Yes	___No
Tithe	X Yes	___No

Here Jesus says to throw away your checklist Christianity. One can pass many of our little status checks and still be far from God. I can have a "quiet time" with little focus on God. I can put in my contribution check the same way I pay the utility bill. Jesus certainly doesn't say to disregard the absolute lines God has drawn because those lines give us boundaries, but boundaries without the heart make a hollow shell.

Absolute Purity

Probably the biggest challenge that I face in my Christian walk is in this text. It is easy to keep the letter of the law and not commit adultery, but lust. . .that is a different matter. It is a daily struggle, one that I probably lose at some point almost every day.

Your daily struggle may not be lust; it may be fear or faithlessness or losing control of your tongue, but you have one. Here Jesus gives us the key to overcoming. He says, *"If your right eye causes you to sin, gouge it out and throw it away."* Ouch! As usual Jesus is radical, far more radical than we are comfortable with. "Come on, Jesus; you can't be serious. Gouge out my eye? Is this a cult you are starting? Who's really going to do that?" And so we try to explain it all away. Jesus' profound point is that I should love God so much and hate sin so much that I will **do anything to keep myself pure**. Jesus is preaching **absolute purity**! I know that gouging out my eye or cutting off my hand will not prevent my lust; but if I am willing to do anything at all to be righteous, including giving up my eyesight, I will find **something**, perhaps just as radical, to overcome my lust.

Why is a sin like lust so harmful that such drastic action must be taken? We need to understand purity. Perhaps this illustration will help. I was sharing a great meal with friends at a restaurant. The appetizers were delicious and so was the salad that I was eating, until. . .I bit into something that I knew shouldn't be in any salad! I took this object out of my mouth and looked—it was a chicken bone, and I wasn't eating chicken salad. Somehow the remains of someone else's garbage had ended up in my salad! It is an understatement to say that the rest of the meal just didn't appeal to me. That is how impurity affects our lives. It may be hidden in the salad; no one else may know it's there, but it spoils the rest of the meal. Continual sin such as impurity is used by Satan to destroy our spiritual appetite. We are filled with guilt; our faith that we can overcome it is damaged; we may compound this sin by hiding it; we are robbed of the victory that Jesus wants us to have.

Conquer Your Sin

How can I gouge out the sin? First, I must understand that Jesus wants us to be perfectly pure. Second, I must be desperate enough to do anything to overcome the sin. Third, I must examine myself and my sin. When am I tempted to lust? What are the catalysts? TV, movies, magazines, books, etc.? When am I tempted? When I am alone, with certain people or in certain places?

Fourth, I need to be open about my sin with another disciple who will love me enough to not let up on me until I have overcome.

If you don't see the need to confess your sin (James 5:16), **you don't yet have the heartfelt conviction to do anything to conquer you sin.** It is embarrassing to be totally open about a sin, especially a sexual sin, that comes up over and over again. But the embarrassment actually helps to overcome. I'm not talking about grudgingly sharing the truth that is pried out of me and hiding or evading the rest, but having a heart that wants to totally expose and kill the sin.

Absolute purity is Jesus' standard; we must make it our standard. Have you? Honestly, have you? It is continual growth in these areas that provides excitement and encouragement that ensures that we will be disciples for the long haul.

AL BAIRD
Los Angeles, Calif.

FOR FURTHER STUDY:

Romans 7:21-25, 12:1-2
1 Corinthians 9:24-27
Colossians 3:5-11
Hebrews 12:1-3

Marriage

True Companions

"It has been said, 'Anyone who divorces his wife must give her a certificate of divorce.' But I tell you that anyone who divorces his wife, except for marital unfaithfulness, causes her to become an adulteress, and anyone who marries the divorced woman commits adultery" (Matthew 5:31-32).

IRRECONCILABLE DIFFERENCES. INCOMPATIBILITY. MENTAL ANGUISH. On-paper reasons for divorce. In-the-heart reason? "I just don't love him/her anymore." Jesus' teaching on divorce is strong. It challenges the fickleness of human nature. A spoiled and pampered people don't know the definition of faithfulness and integrity in the marriage relationship.

Because of its teaching on divorce, the Bible is dismissed by many. In the United States and other countries the word "divorce" is as commonly used as "marriage," and is widely accepted and even encouraged. Interestingly, human nature has not changed much in 2,000 years. In one of their confrontations with Jesus (Matthew 19:3), the Pharisees tested him by asking, *"Is it lawful for a man to divorce his wife for any and every reason?"* In that day a man could divorce his wife if she did anything he disliked—even if she burned his food while cooking it! The husband cried the first century equivalent of "irreconcilable differences" and got a new wife.

Jesus' response is found in Matthew 5:31-32 and in 19:1-9. In the latter passage Jesus lays the foundation for his teaching on divorce—God's original and perfect plan. One man—one woman—one lifetime. God's way works! Complete faithfulness in marriage. Go in the front door of marriage and keep the back door shut. Go in with a mindset of giving of yourself, of meeting his/her needs, of working through conflict, of staying **put** through the rough times, of not giving up.

Marriage as an Analogy

Faithfulness. If we truly have it in marriage, we must first have it with God. The Scriptures repeatedly draw a parallel between marriage and our relationship with God. As Jesus recalled God's plan for marriage from the beginning (Matthew 19:5, Genesis 2:24), he used the word "united." Romans 6:5 conveys the reality of being "united" with Christ in his death and in his resurrection. The *oneness* in marriage is also stressed in our relationship with Christ—*"for you are all one in Christ Jesus"* (Galatians 3:28). Paul in his letter to the church in Ephesus uses the identical statement found in Genesis 2:24 and Matthew 19:5 in his instructions to husbands and wives. Then in Ephesians 5:32 he clarifies the correlation, *"This is a profound mystery—but I am talking about Christ and the church."*

Unfaithfulness in marriage is also unfaithfulness to God! 1John 4:20 says *". . .for anyone who does not love his brother, whom he has seen, cannot love God, whom he has not seen."* In much the same way, how can man claim to be faithful to God and not be faithful to his spouse? This principle is clear as God communicates his displeasure through Malachi 2:14, *". . .the Lord is acting as the witness between you and the wife of your youth, because you have broken faith with her, though she is your partner, the wife of your marriage covenant."* It is amazing to see how integral God's spiritual principles are to our human relationships. Our faithfulness to him is mirrored in our faithfulness to our husbands/wives.

Marriage as a Model

In a time when half of all marriages end in divorce (and even more couples are emotionally divorced) what a privilege it is to be disciples of Jesus. Disciples whose marriages can be used by God as lights and examples. Godly models of strong marriages are more vital than ever. I am eternally grateful for the example of my parents' God-centered marriage of 60 years. Their devotion and love for God and each other continue to inspire my husband Al and me as we grow in our marriage. As our daughters marry, we see the incredible impact of discipling. And now, at the recent birth of our first granddaughter, we envision the plan for great Christian marriages going on and on.

What kind of model is your marriage? Is it a model of faithfulness or unfaithfulness? Nothing tests our marriages like seeing the reality of discipling lived out in the marriages of our children and others watching us. We may not realize that we are teaching others through our marriages. But we are—either positively or negatively. Praying together has been the spiritual "glue" that bonds our marriage. Daily prayer has kept us open and vulnerable to God and to each other. Our unity of heart, mind and purpose have been intensified in those special times together.

Do you want others to imitate the unity and oneness in your marriage? Are you working as a team, or do you have your own separate agendas? There are times Al senses "resistance" from me is some area. Disunity in our team hurts us both. If we get "off-track" emotionally or sexually, it weakens our effectiveness as a team and makes us more vulnerable to Satan's temptations. If either of us loses our concern for others, the strength of our unity is lessened. Unity can be destroyed by unresolved conflict, bitterness, lack of forgiveness and just plain apathy.

Satan desires to strike deadly blows to our faithfulness. He eagerly goes after it. Daily. Always. No vacation. Only as we choose to adhere to God's standard will our marriages bring glory to God.

At weddings, the question is "Will you forsake all others and be faithful till death parts you?" At divorces, the judge asks, "Is your marriage irretrievably broken with no hope of reconciliation?" Many have said, "Yes!" to the first question. Half of those have also said, "Yes!" to the second question. The fullness of the tragedy is that so many in both groups have never said, "Yes!" to God. They have not built their marriages on a foundation of true faithfulness. Disciples of Jesus, who have been made new through the blood of Christ, can joyfully and gratefully say, "Yes!" to being faithful in marriage. Daily. Always. Forever.

GLORIA BAIRD
Los Angeles, Calif.

FOR FURTHER STUDY:

Deuteronomy 24:1-4
Hosea 4:10-14
Malachi 2:13-16
Mark 10:11-12
Luke 16:18
Hebrews 13:4

If You Don't Mean It, Don't Say It

"Simply let your 'Yes' be 'Yes,' and your 'No,' 'No,' anything beyond this comes from the evil one" (Matthew 5:37).

THE SERMON ON THE MOUNT IS ABOUT BEING DIFFERENT. IN JESUS' most famous discourse, he is constantly contrasting the flashy but fatal with the radical he calls right. Two roads are clearly laid out—the happy and the sad, the light and the darkness, the wise and the foolish, the honest and the false. How easy it would have been to leave out integrity with our tongue. Jesus didn't leave it out. In fact, he camped on it for awhile and called it devilish to be deceitful.

A Long Run?

Listen to this story about a woman who left out of her life what Jesus preached was essential. She crossed the finish line first. It was one of the most prestigious races in the world. A wreath was placed on her head. The TV cameras rolled as sportscasters praised her incredible rise from unknown to champion. The year was 1980 and Rosie Ruiz had won the Boston Marathon.

Or had she? Very soon after Ruiz broke the tape, accusations began to fly challenging the legitimacy of her victory. She didn't look as if she had run an entire marathon. No one remembered even seeing her on the course. Finally, some spectators charged her with entering the race at the 25-mile mark. She was ultimately stripped of her title.

The most incredible part of the story, however, is that to this day she has claimed innocence. She vowed to run another marathon and prove her ability. She never did. She said she would convince psychologists of her claim. She could not. In fact, they called this bright, articulate, seemingly balanced woman a sociopath.

What's the point? Very simple. We have all got a bit of Rosie Ruiz in us. We love the applause of people. We even desire an ovation in heaven before the angels. We want to win the crown and stand as victors before the nations on that great day. Unfortunately, we don't want to run every step of the race to get it. We are unhappy but paralyzed by the fear of getting caught. So we close up and clam up. We have been diagnosed—a religiopath.

A Little Thing?

The people of Jesus' day wanted to get to heaven. They thought too of the *"well done good and faithful servant"* speech. But it's the little things, each challenge of the marathon we call life that will eventually make or break us. The half-brother of Jesus put it this way, *"If anyone considers himself religious and yet does not keep a tight rein on his tongue, he deceives himself and his religion is worthless"* (James 1:26). There is nothing more important eternally than that "little thing" called the tongue.

Jesus walked into the religious games of his day and simplified life. He chastised the smug Jew who believed that as long as you referred to God's name, your vow was binding but leaving out his name meant you could leave out the fulfillment. Wasn't God present even if his name wasn't called? Don't you really need to tell the truth even when you cross your fingers?

Let's ask Paul what the most important ingredient in a true disciple is. Is it loving? Serving? Sincerity? Here's what he told Timothy: *"And the things you have heard me say in the presence of many witnesses entrust to reliable men who will also be qualified to teach others"* (2 Timothy 2:2). Paul's character emphasis was first and foremost on reliability. It only makes sense. An unreliable man will not only break God's chain for disciple-making but will also discourage others from continuing to run their races.

The most obvious way we can be unreliable is with our tongue. In Psalm 5:9 David said of his adversaries, *"Not a word from their mouth can be trusted. . . ."* With their lips, a "yes" had become a "no." Our Bible says that has only one source, the evil one.

How about us? We say, "I'll pray for you." Do we? We say, "I'll have you over to eat." Did we? We promise, "See you at 7:30." Was it more like 8:00? "But I had a legitimate excuse," you say. Did you call? Were you reliable with your lips?

You see, it's not just the heathen world that has tongue trouble. An irate prophet scorched religious, but disobedient, Israel with this, *"Truth has perished; it has vanished from their lips"* (Jeremiah

7:28). David also went after his people in Psalm 52:3, *"You love evil rather than good, falsehood rather than speaking the truth."* Our religious lies, like the Jews', are generally not blatant. And yet how easy it is for us to exaggerate the facts for our benefit. How smoothly we slide into deceit that conveniently leaves something out. We have stopped running the race and bought into the death trap of the father of lies (John 8:44).

Neither Corrupt nor Negligent

Quit playing swearing games, our Lord demands. Get a character that speaks and lives the truth. Our "no" is okay if we say "no." Many of us need to learn not to accept more than we can live up to. We have set ourselves up to be unreliable.

But mostly it should and can be "yes" in Jesus (2 Corinthians 1:19). Take on new frontiers. Go help the poor. Get moving and lead somebody. Say "yes" and live "yes."

We praise God for many heroes who then and now have lived out his "yes." Daniel lived such a consistent life that even his enemies were astonished. *"They could find no corruption in him, because he was trustworthy and neither corrupt nor negligent. Finally these men said, 'We will never find any basis for charges against this man. . .'"* (Daniel 6:4-5).

As in all areas, Jesus is our best example. Perhaps his favorite phrase was, *"I tell you the truth."* He did and he does. He predicted his death for us. That marathon got very tough. He desired to back out of those words. There were even reasons to break his pledge. But Jesus, as always, delivered. His "yes" was "yes," and we are so grateful. How about your "yes"?

JIMMY AND ANITA ALLEN
Worcester, Mass.

FOR FURTHER STUDY:

Psalm 39:1-3
Proverbs 16:20-27
2 Corinthians 1:15-22
James 3:1-12, 5:12

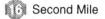

Above (and Beyond) the Law

"You have heard that it was said, 'Eye for eye, and tooth for tooth.' But I tell you, Do not resist an evil person. If someone strikes you on the right cheek, turn to him the other also. And if someone wants to sue you and take your tunic, let him have your cloak as well. If someone forces you to go one mile, go with him two miles. Give to the one who asks you, and do not turn away from the one who wants to borrow from you" (Matthew 5:38-42).

A LITTLE BOY AND HIS YOUNGER SISTER WERE RIDING A HOBBY horse together. The boy said, " If one of us would just get off this horse, there would be more room for me." Ever meet any adults like him? We are often repulsed by the self-centeredness that surrounds us. However, we can't deny that as Christians we struggle to avoid being controlled by it as well. This passage is a strong call to an attitude of selflessness that Jesus Christ expects to see in all disciples.

Retaliation, Legal Rights, and the Second Mile

Jesus first addresses the desire to retaliate for injury done to us and calls us to rid ourselves of it. In Exodus 21:24 we find an eye for an eye, and a tooth for a tooth which was originally written to control excess violence and the desire for revenge. There was a tendency then, as there is today, for an individual when harmed to not only hit back but go beyond, even to the point of killing. It was this excess that the law was striving to stop. The object was not to urge men to take an eye for an eye and a tooth for a tooth and to insist upon it, but to justly see that the punishment fit the crime. Jesus taught that *"if someone strikes you on the right cheek, turn to him the other also."* This would require the power and conviction to restrain oneself.

Jesus next addresses the tendency for us to insist upon our legal rights. Jesus gives the example of a man coming to sue another in a court of law for his inner garment. According to Jewish law he could never be sued for his outer garment though it was legitimate to sue for an inner one. Instead of maintaining the stance of "I must have my rights" Jesus calls us to another standard. He is making the point that our main concern should not be with personal rights but with justice, righteousness and truth (see John 18:19-24).

Lastly he addresses the issue of going the second mile. By law the Roman government, and in particular the Roman army, had the right to commandeer a man at any place and require him to carry a certain amount of baggage to another place. Then they could take hold of someone else and force him to do the same. Such a law and its frequent use caused great resentment among the Jews who felt deeply the Romans should have no rights over them at all. Jesus' teaching that one should carry the baggage not only the first mile but a second as well surely was a shock to those who heard it. This was a radical sermon! Jesus was saying go beyond what is required by the authorities. Certainly the spirit of Jesus' message condemns *any* resentment we may feel against a legitimate authority.

If reform seems necessary, the Bible doesn't teach that we are not to seek change (see 1 Corinthians 7:21-23). Change, however, must always be sought by lawful means or not at all. The Jew who would not only go the first mile but a second (with a smile) would indeed be a rare individual. He would be someone who would cause others to wonder by what power could he be so different. Jesus himself went that second mile—*"Very rarely will anyone die for a righteous man, though for a good man someone might possibly dare to die. But God demonstrates his own love for us in this: while we were still sinners, Christ died for us"* (Romans 5:7-8). Jesus led the way and we are called to follow.

The Power of Example

A disciple I know who is an architect began a project under the supervision of a non-Christian boss some time ago. On this job the disciple was always found to be reliable and forthright. He made it clear to others that he was deeply committed to God in addition to his work. His boss was struck by his tendency to maintain his focus at all times and not get involved in worldly conversation in the office. He saw him being concerned about people as well as the job to be done. He always saw him taking on deadlines and added responsibilities with a good attitude. He noticed tremendous persistence in tackling his projects. It was about this time that the disciple shared his faith with the boss. Though the boss had become a complacent religious individual, he responded to an invitation to look more seriously at the Bible. Not only did he study the Bible, but his wife did as well, and a few months ago with a disciple's commitment, they were both baptized into Jesus Christ. The boss saw in the disciple an attitude of going the second mile.

The questions for us are: (1) How do we respond to demands placed on us by the authorities over us, and (2) do we tend to always look to defend our personal rights as a matter of priority in our lives? The authorities over us, whether they are governmental, employer, teacher, parent, or church are from God. Some of us still have trouble with the first mile. Jesus was the supreme "second miler," and we must realize that the world will be turned upside down only by "second milers." Specifically, how can you be one today, this week, on your job, in your home, in your town? Don't hold back. Don't stop with the first mile. Go above and beyond.

DOUGLAS WEBBER, M.D.
Boston, Mass.

FOR FURTHER STUDY:

1 Corinthians 6:1-8
1 Corinthians 7:21-23
I Corinthians 9:19-23
Colossians 3:22-25
1 Peter 2:13-17

Not Kidding

"You have heard that it was said, 'Love your neighbor and hate your enemy.'
But I tell you: Love your enemies and pray for those who persecute you, that
you may be sons of your Father in heaven. He causes his sun to rise on the
evil and the good, and sends rain on the righteous and the unrighteous. . . .
Be perfect, therefore, as your heavenly Father is perfect" (Matthew 5:43-48).

DID YOU EVER HEAR IT SAID OF SOMEONE, "HE DIDN'T HAVE AN enemy in the world?" Might someone say that about you? Many people mean it as a compliment. But no one ever said that about Jesus. He had enemies, and he fully expected that all those who followed him would have them as well. If you have none, then you're not yet living like Jesus.

But when Jesus talked about enemies he said things you almost never hear anyone say. He used words we normally reserve for family and close friends. He used the word "love." And he wasn't kidding. Jesus *is* radical.

Being like God

His challenge to love our enemies and to pray for our persecutors smashed the religious *status quo* of his day, and it does nothing different to the norms of our day. His message totally defies worldly standards. It pushes us to the limit. Will we imitate God or mirror the world? Behind this radical call is God! God is love. His perfect, steadfast nature continues to bestow blessings regardless of the recipient. God loves the worst of sinners as much as the most faithful of disciples. That's incredible, but what is even more incredible is that Jesus calls us to be like God and nothing less. What a challenge! Imagine imitating God. That is exactly what Jesus demands.

Consider the alternative: Responding like the world, so often pitifully enslaved by how others treat them. Loving people who love them back, but critical, bitter, resentful, vengeful towards people that mistreat them. Regardless of how much we may love the brotherhood, any bitterness or resentment in our hearts towards our persecutors simply reduces us to the level of the world. Shall we conform to the hearts of wicked men? Shall we follow in their footsteps? After Jesus' costly sacrifice on the cross, have we still learned nothing?

Showing Who We Are

No matter how painful or unjust the treatment, we must prove to be sons of God and not pawns of Satan. The pain is real but God's grace is sufficient (2 Corinthians 12:7-9). This enables us to glorify God and shine brightly in a dark world.In light of all this, what does Jesus expect? First, he expects us to have enemies. He doesn't expect us to go out determined to make enemies, but he calls us to mitate his life which will produce the same kinds of enemies that he had. How many people have slandered or threatened us lately? How many names of enemies quickly come to mind? Any delay in thinking must alarm us! Are we really having an impact for Jesus? Are we willing to go all the way and suffer for him (Philippians 1:29)? I remember wrestling with this conviction years ago while living in a third world country. One day during a major religious festival, I was standing on the side of a dusty street waiting to catch a bus to an early morning meeting of disciples. That day vividly stands out in my mind because I was literally being engulfed by thousands of religious zealots in flowing robes who were embarked on a pilgrimage. As I stood there with my black leather Bible,blue jeans and blonde hair, the reality of taking a stand for Jesus Christ poignantly sank in. Was I willing to pay the price?

To be a disciple means to go all the way for Jesus in whatever country or culture we are in. We need to reach out to many people and get involved in their lives whether they like it or not. With how many people are we presently studying the Bible? How do we act around family, friends and peers? Are we boldly speaking the truth in love? Do we confront sin? Or do we hold back waiting for another time or another person to take responsibility? Now is the time for every disciple to get involved in the mission on a daily basis and be prepared for the enemies who will certainly show up.

Secondly, Jesus expects us to love and actively pray for the people who oppose us. After only eight months in the previously mentioned country, I recall disciples gathering every morning, praying and begging God to soften the hearts of the local religious leaders who were threatening to expel us. As we prayed daily for them by name, God began to fill our hearts with compassion, enabling us to want only the very best for them. Instead of reacting like the world, we persisted in loving people like the Father.

Living in Cambodia has discipled my heart radically to meet the unique needs of people scarred by decades of civil war, genocide, political unrest, hatred and poverty. God has discipled me through many challenges.

In particular, one sharp young convert that I once discipled became an enemy of the church. God had revealed considerable pride, envy and ingratitude in his heart. Instead of repenting, he became quite resistant and vindictive, sowing doubts among other Cambodian disciples and speaking divisive words about the leaders. For nearly one year, the staff and I poured out our hearts, love and trust to that brother, only to have it misconstrued and trampled on. The pain was deep. After he left, I praised God for protecting the church, but I pitied my former friend for his lost state. I still pray that one day he will be saved.

How much do we persevere with people? Do we answer back kindly when spoken to unjustly? We need to crucify the sinful nature and love like God no matter how much it hurts, praying that one day our very persecutors might join us, willing also to be persecuted for the name of Christ.

MARK REMIJAN
Phnom Penh, Cambodia

FOR FURTHER STUDY:

2 Samuel 16:5-14, 19:18-23
Matthew 23:37-39
Mark 6:14-29
Luke 23:26-43
1 Corinthians 4:9-16

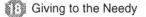

Keeping a Sweet Secret

"Be careful not to do your 'acts of righteousness' before men, to be seen by them. If you do, you will have no reward from your Father in heaven. So when you give to the needy, do not announce it with trumpets, as the hypocrites do in the synagogues and on the streets, to be honored by men. I tell you the truth, they have received their reward in full. But when you give to the needy, do not let your left hand know what your right hand is doing, so that your giving may be in secret. Then your Father, who sees what is done in secret, will reward you" (Matthew 6:1-4).

IT WAS ONCE A HIGH SCHOOL, FULL OF ENERGETIC CAMBODIAN teenagers preparing for the future. Now it is called the "Tuol Sleng Museum of Crime." Converted into an interrogation and torture center by the radical Khmer Rouge guerrillas from 1975-1979, it was used to rob those same teenagers and their families of any future at all. Of the estimated 12,000 people who entered, only **seven** survived! First you see the interrogation rooms with photographs of the last victims. They were found shackled to metal beds, their stomachs bloated, body parts exposed and mutilated, lying in a pool of their own dried blood. The second building consists of three floors of detention cells encased in barbed wire to prevent suicide attempts. In the third building, thousands of pictures crowd the walls telling a ghastly tale: a woman is whipped as her children watch; a man is strangled to death as another soldier breaks his arms and legs; a man's fingernails are forcibly pulled out; another is shackled and submerged, drowning to death; and another is so weak and emaciated that he has to be carried on a wooden pole by two men to his interrogation session. Babies are tossed into the air and bayoneted to death while others are taken by the legs and bashed against a tree to crack their skulls. To visit a place like this leaves you completely overwhelmed and speechless.

Taking Personal Responsibility

In a poor, devastated country like Cambodia, the needs of the people cry out. God's call for us to give rings loud and clear. But, regardless of where we live, people in need surround us. Underlying Jesus' teaching on how to give is the assumption that we are already giving. How sensitive are you to the needs of others? Do you make a personal effort to find out how to love your neighbor, or do you wait for others to initiate? Are you more comfortable when you don't know the needs so that you don't have to feel responsible? Worse still, are you so blinded that you cannot see beyond your own personal needs? Remember, even the Son of Man came to serve and to give his life! (Matthew 20:28). We need to start giving to others like our Lord Jesus Christ did!

In Matthew 6:1-4 Jesus teaches us how to give. We must give in secret, without even those closest to us knowing about it. God himself gives in secret. He blesses even the unrighteous and ungrateful (Matthew 5:45). God gives because he wants to. Do you give in secret? How many times have you felt hurt or even struggled when your giving was not acknowledged? Are you content when no one but God sees your sacrifice? Do you give without wanting anything in return and lend without expecting to be paid back (Luke 6:30)?

Giving Means Sacrifice

There is a Christian in Cambodia whose husband abandoned her with four children and an orphaned niece to support. She is sick and could possibly have cancer. Her teacher's salary is not enough to live on. She often walks to church. When I went to visit her one day, I found out that she lives about three miles away from the church meeting place on a dirt road that floods up to the waist during heavy rains. Yet, I have never heard her complain or talk about her own needs. She always comes to church happy and ready to encourage others. She sacrifices in secret and focuses on the needs of others! Her reward will be great in heaven!

Jesus' life was one of sacrificial giving and he expects us to do likewise. In Luke 21:1-4 he lifts up the widow for giving out of her poverty. She gave all she had to live on! She totally trusted God. Then in Matthew 19:21, Jesus challenges the rich young man to sell everything and give to the poor. Jesus tells him to give it all. He calls him to be like God. John 3:16 says that "God so loved. . .that he gave his one and only Son." God gave his greatest treasure. How it must have hurt God to see how we treated Jesus. What pain God must have felt to see the flogging and mocking and beating and finally to see his son on the cross crying out in agony. And then He turned away and abandoned him to death in order to meet the needs of the world. What perfect love! "If you want to be perfect," Jesus tells the rich young man, "go, sell out, and give!" Jesus tells us not to have a grabby, possessive heart, but to have a giving, sharing heart. Anything less means we are not worthy to be his disciples. To be sacrificial is a decision we make every day if we are to walk as Jesus did.

Having been a disciple for many years, I have seen how easy it can be to give out of emotional reaction rather than daily decision. We feel moved to give after seeing a powerful video presentation or hearing a heartfelt testimony, but it doesn't last. Are we just one-time givers or daily givers? Have we made sacrifice a lifestyle or a knee-jerk reaction to the conviction of our leaders? Have we grown so comfortable that an actual lowering of our lifestyle is difficult to do? Let us not give as the world does but as Jesus does!

Giving must be a decision we make, and we must do it with joy. 2 Corinthians 9:7 says God **loves** a cheerful giver. Can you imagine that? God is looking down from heaven and he just loves it when we give joyfully, sacrificially, secretly and when we are just thankful for the opportunity to be like him. It warms his heart to see us meeting the needs of others out of our own gratitude to him. He rejoices when we have his heart for the needy—physically, emotionally or spiritually. Out of his joy, he rewards us with all spiritual blessings in Christ Jesus—now and forever. We can never outgive our gracious God. Let us work for this reward and show the world that we are truly **his** disciples!

PATSY REMIJAN
Phnom Penh, Cambodia

FOR FURTHER STUDY:

Luke 6:30-38
John14:27
2 Corinthians 8:1-9, 9:6-15
Hebrews 6:10

Handle Prayerfully

"And when you pray, do not be like the hypocrites, for they love to pray standing in the synagogues and on the street corners to be seen by men. I tell you the truth, they have received their reward in full. But when you pray, go into your room, close the door and pray to your Father, who is unseen. Then your Father, who sees what is done in secret, will reward you. And when you pray, do not keep on babbling like pagans, for they think they will be heard because of their many words. Do not be like them, for your Father knows what you need before you ask him. "This, then, is how you should pray. . ." (Matthew 6:5-15).

P OWER. PEACE. PURITY. PERCEPTION. THE POWER TO CHANGE radically. The peace that passes all understanding. A purity that surpasses that of the Pharisees. The perception that comes down from heaven. As we strive daily to imitate our Lord, don't we long to be filled with these fruits of God's Spirit?

Jesus was a powerful man. He was a man always at peace with his Father. He led a totally sinless life. His perceptions and insights were wise and wonderful! Jesus was a man of prayer. He prayed for the power to heal and to change others (Mark 9:29). He wrestled in prayer in order to be at peace with God's will (Matthew 26:36-46). He struggled in prayer to be wholeheartedly submissive to his Father (Hebrews 5:7-8). Jesus prayed by himself (Matthew 14:23) and before others (John 11:41-43). He prayed with his face to the ground (Matthew 26:39) and looking up towards heaven (John 17:1). He prayed standing up (Mark 11:25), kneeling down (Luke 22:41), early in the morning (Mark 1:35) and through the night (Luke 6:12).

Jesus expects each disciple to imitate his prayer life. In his powerful Sermon on the Mount he does not begin his teaching on prayer with the words "If you pray" or "Please, I beg you to pray" or "I command you to pray." He very simply says, *"When you pray"* (Matthew 6:5). Jesus knows that we will pray. He knows that we will need to pray. So he takes the time here to teach us how to pray.

Not like the Hypocrites

Jesus' first challenge to our prayer life is to "Be Real!" The hypocrites were those who honored God with their lips, but their hearts were far from him (Matthew 15:8). They were those who prayed because it helped their spiritual image. It appeased their consciences. It was the religious thing to do. The purpose of a disciple's prayer life is to keep him honestly, emotionally and wholeheartedly knit together with God his Father each and every day. Are you genuinely struggling with God in order to submit to him as a disciple on a daily basis? Are you as honest with God when you don't want to do his will as Jesus was in the garden (Matthew 26:36-46)? How deeply do you wrestle with God through life's disappointments, hurts and tragedies? Do you call out to God with loud cries and tears as you learn submission through times of challenge and suffering? We must never let religious words and actions characterize our prayer life. Remember, do not be like the hypocrites. Instead, be real with your God.

In Your Room

Secondly we are challenged to find a place to pray. Jesus wants us to be isolated so that without interruption (from children or roommates) and without distraction (by the telephone, the laundry or our homework) we can be alone with God. We can pray out loud. We can talk, laugh, sing, shout, cry or whisper. We feel more freedom to be ourselves and to be deeply honest. Whether it's your bedroom, a closet, a field or a forest, Jesus wants us to be alone with the Father.

No Babbling

Clear-minded. Personal. That's what Jesus wants us to be in our prayers. Who babbles? Two-year-olds, nervous people, worried people, "spacy" people, lazy-minded people, superficial people and self-conscious people. Pagans, who do not know God and are living to please themselves, pray like this. When you pray, are you worrying out loud? Are you complaining to God and asking him to meet your needs and satisfy your desires? Or are you thoughtful, faithful and outwardly focused as you pray for yourself, the Kingdom and the lost world? A disciple in prayer should be confident, at peace, clear minded, alert, deep and focused on others. And if he is having trouble with any of these qualities, he is real and honest and repentant before God.

When You Pray, Say:

How to pray. More than a checklist. A glimpse into the heart of one who communicated perfectly with the Father. Jesus blesses us with specific teaching on how to pray (Matthew 6:9-13). If we will follow the outline of Jesus and seek to imitate the heart of Jesus, we will have deep and effective prayer lives.

1. *Our Father in Heaven*: Begin by setting our minds on the personal and intimate relationship we have with our God.

2. *Hallowed be your name*: Praise and honor him.

3. *Your Kingdom come*: Pray for his Kingdom, the church—specifically for the Christians in our lives and the leaders of our local church family and for Christians and leaders in other places. Pray for those to whom his Kingdom has not come—people who need to become disciples of Jesus.

4. *Your will be done*: Pray for a submissive heart to the will of God for your life—whatever it may be.

5. *Give us this day our daily bread*: Pray through today's schedule. Trust God to meet your needs. Pray to rely on him today and not on yourself.

6. *Forgive us our debts*: Specific confession of sin.

7. *As we also have forgiven our debtors*: Commit before God to resolve any hurts, attitudes, conflicts or concerns in any and all of your relationships.

8. *Lead us not into temptation*: Wrestle with God to be submissive and repentant in your particular areas of weakness.

9. *Deliver us from the evil one*: Pray that God ties
Satan's hands. Thank God for the victories that he
has won and those that he will win!

Power, peace, purity and perception are the fruits of a great prayer life. When we pray... we are to imitate the Master. When we pray... our Father in heaven will reward us! Let us all pray, every day. Let us all pray honestly, personally, purposefully and specifically. And the will of God will be done on earth as it is in heaven.

ADRIENNE SCANLON
Paris, France

FOR FURTHER STUDY:

John 17:1-26
Philippians 1:3-11
1 Thessalonians 5:16-24
James 5:13-20
1 Peter 4:7-11

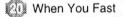

Hunger and Humility

"When you fast, do not look somber as the hypocrites do, for they disfigure their faces to show men they are fasting. I tell you the truth, they have received their reward in full. But when you fast, put oil on your head and wash your face, so that it will not be obvious to men that you are fasting, but only to your Father, who is unseen; and your Father, who sees what is done in secret, will reward you" (Matthew 6:16-18).

I
T IS SAID THAT THE QUICKEST WAY TO A MAN'S HEART IS THROUGH his stomach. The constant flow of strawberry tarts and chocolate chip cookies coming my way when I was dating my wife Adrienne certainly paved the way to my heart. The Bible appeals to husbands that they should love their wives as their own bodies, reasoning that, *"after all, no one ever hated his own body, but he feeds it and cares for it."* Isn't that the truth? We do like to feed our bodies!

For some of us, it's a question of quantity: Mind-boggling portions followed by seconds. For others, consistency is important: Three square meals a day never missing the mid-afternoon and before bedtime snacks. In France, quality is king. After living in Paris for several years, I began to see "gastronomy" as the highest form of art, something to be appreciated, respected and savored, not just devoured. Whatever your point of view, we all love to eat.

Right in the Gut

Then Jesus hits us right where we live. In the middle of the greatest sermon ever preached he says: *"When you fast..."* (Matthew 6:16). A friend once told me that he was "fasting from television for a week." Though his intentions were good and the discipline surely helpful, the fact remains that "to fast means primarily "not to eat" (Greek *nesteuo*, from *ne*, a negative prefix, and *esthio*, to eat). That's certainly what Jesus means. And notice that he says "When you fast" and not "If you fast." I must admit that even several years into my Christian life I would have expected fasting to be addressed in Matthew 5 in the following manner: "You have heard that it was said to the people long ago 'Ye shall fasteth,' but I tell you, Don't worry about it." And yet, if Jesus expects every disciple to give (6:2) and to pray (6:3) (and he does!), then he fully expects fasting to be a part of the life of every disciple. When questioned by the Pharisees about the subject, Jesus replied, *"The time will come when the bridegroom will be taken away from them; then they will fast."* Well, Jesus has gone back to the Father, and it's high time we started fasting as he intended.

When was the last time you fasted? And before that? And the time before? Why don't we fast more than we do? David says in Psalm 35:13, *"I humbled myself with fasting."* Humility—what we need the most and want the least. Much of the fasting recorded in the Scriptures is associated with confession and repentance of sin. Isn't that humbling? Fasting reminds us of how frail our physical bodies really are. Isn't it humbling to feel weak after two days of fasting? Fasting also reveals the weakness of our spiritual will to master certain simple physical desires. Isn't it humbling to have to struggle to not eat a stupid piece of cake?

Fasting tests our earnestness to move God to action, forcing us to admit that sometimes prayer alone may not suffice (Mark 9:29). God desires to humble us, not to beat us down, but in order to lift us up. He wants us to learn the power of discipline and self-control, and become truly spiritual.

The problem is that we can totally miss the point and that's why Jesus talks about our motivation. Fasting is one of the "acts of righteousness" (6:1) in which we must surpass the righteousness of the Pharisees (5:20). In my mind, there are few things more pitiful that a Christian trying to impress other men. It's always interesting to watch someone who's fasting when he's offered food. He may simply respond, "No, thank you," or come right out, "I'm fasting." Jesus is not saying we cannot share our spiritual experience, but check your heart. While you may refrain from making a public announcement, are you hoping others will find out and be impressed by you and your commitment? If so, you have already received your reward in full. Don't expect any more from God.

God asks his people in Zechariah 7:5, *"...was it really for me that you fasted?"* How often do you fast "in secret" to "your Father who is unseen"? For many, the majority of our fasts are done with the church or a smaller group. But collective fasting is like collective prayer: It's a good thing, but it doesn't replace a personal relationship with God. Forget impressing others. Don't just do it for the personal benefits. Fast to God. And he will reward you.

Practical Matters

So where do we begin? How can we take it higher? Throughout the centuries, men and women of God have fasted at various times, in a variety of ways, for a multitude of reasons. Jesus fasted for 40 days (Matthew 4:2), Paul for three days (Acts 9:9), and the Israelites one day at Mizpah (1 Samuel 7:6). Jesus did not eat, but apparently drank water. Ezra ate no food and drank no water (Ezra 10:6). Daniel ate no choice food (meat or wine) for three weeks (Daniel 10:3). Keep it spiced up with variety. Call yourself higher. Always do it for God. The leaders in Antioch (Acts 13:3) fasted before beginning a new mission. Paul fasted during his conversion. Why not fast to God for someone you hope to win to Christ? Moses (Exodus 34:28) and Daniel (Daniel 10:3) fasted while receiving the word of God to communicate to the people. How about a day of fasting and Bible study to gain greater insight and conviction?

At those moments when we become aware of our need to radically change in an area of our lives, let's humble ourselves with fasting to God. Be it for several days or a couple of weeks, let's confess our sin and cry out to God in prayer for a period of time. And our Father who sees what is done in secret will surely reward us, to his glory.

BRIAN SCANLON
Paris, France

FOR FURTHER STUDY :

Ezra 10:1-6
Isaiah 58:1-9
Joel 1:13-20, 2:12-14
Luke 18:9-14

Part 3

Principle

Wise Investing

"Do not store up for yourselves treasures on earth, where moth and rust destroy, and where thieves break in and steal. But store up for yourselves treasures in heaven, where moth and rust do not destroy, and where thieves do not break in and steal. For where your treasure is, there your heart will be also" (Matthew 6:19-21).

Y OU KNOW THE COMMANDMENTS: READ YOUR BIBLE; PRAY every morning; share your faith; be a good disciple. . . ." "All these I have kept since I was baptized," he replied. "You still lack one thing. Sell your possessions and give to the poor. Then you will have treasure in heaven."

This could be the modern day version of the parable of the rich young man. Jesus is not interested in our obeying him outwardly without having our hearts set on heaven. In Hebrews 11 Abraham was commended for *"looking forward to a city with foundations, whose architect and builder is God"(v.10).* All of the ancients were applauded as those who were *"longing for a better country— a heavenly one."* And the Bible says that God is, therefore, *"not ashamed to be called their God"(v.16).*

Real Treasure

Living the Christian life means much more than living up to a standard of behavior. It has always meant asking deeper questions of motivation and heart with an understanding that if the heart were properly motivated then the actions would always follow. If we really had the attitude deep in our hearts that we are but aliens on this earth then our commitment to God would be much more consistent and much more radical.

It is commanded that we develop an attitude and heart that does not store up treasure here on earth, because our earthly treasures can be destroyed or stolen. Our treasure in heaven, however, can never fade, spoil or perish.

Let's face reality. A husband works overtime and saves up for a new silk outfit for his wife, only to find that an insect destroyed it while they slept. Thousands of dollars are spent on a brand new car and four years later, just as you finish paying for it, it is already showing signs of rust, decay or engine failure. You save for a stereo, enjoy it for a time only to find one morning that a thief has broken into your house, unplugged and carried off your musical joy. Jesus makes a strong case that it does not make sense to be consumed with treasures here on earth because they will not even last here.

In contrast to fading earthly treasure is our salvation, which is well described in 1 Peter 1:3-4: *"Praise be to the God and Father of our Lord Jesus Christ! In his great mercy he has given us new birth into a living hope through the resurrection of Jesus Christ from the dead, and into an inheritance that can never perish, spoil or fade— kept in heaven for you...."* No moth, no rust, no thief, not even Satan himself can diminish our treasure in heaven. As powerful as Satan is to destroy things on earth, he is powerless to cause our salvation to fade. No wonder Peter says that knowledge of this salvation fills us with an *"inexpressible and glorious joy..."* (1 Peter 1:8). It is incredibly freeing to truly understand that our citizenship is in heaven. It takes away so many worries and allows us to be focused on things that matter, like saving the souls of men. It also gives us an incredible joy to know that our greatest treasure is intact and that no force in heaven or on earth can touch it or take it away.

Home Is Where the Heart Is

It was August 1992, our daughter had not yet turned two, and we were landing in Boston to move back to the States. It was Amira's fifth home, third country and third language. Some might think that she would be insecure having moved so much and changed relationships so often. However, the opposite is true. She loves people and is very well adjusted. My great joy in life is when she asks mommy or daddy if we are going to invite the people at the next table to come to church with us. I remember her at the age of one and a half going down the aisle of a trolley in Milan handing out invitations in Italian. I remember her at the age of three in Zurich handing out invitations in German and being concerned as to how many people would be coming with us to church. I want my daughter and son to have the Kingdom of God on their hearts more than anything else because it alone will last. I have a strong desire to see them grow up without the trappings of materialism. That is really a challenge to me, because more than anything else my children will develop my heart and not my words.

To check and see whether your treasure is in heaven or on earth, ask yourself the following: Will you miss a mid-week service to get that overtime in? Would you move away from a strong church because the money is so much better and "a good church is not *that* far away"? What about your attitude on Sunday? Do your children see a joyful parent excited about the Kingdom of God? What about when it is time for a contribution for a special need—missions or the poor? Are you someone who is described by others as always joyful? When things are difficult, do you get down and want to quit? These questions really expose our hearts and show the true location of our treasure.

Jesus says we can decide where to invest, and then our hearts will follow that investment. Make some decisions today about investing in heaven. Invest all you have and all you are (Romans 12:1). Stay with that investment over the long term, and it will bring you joy. It will never perish, spoil or fade.

BOB TRANCHELL
Boston, Mass.

FOR FURTHER STUDY:

Matthew 6:19-34
Luke 12:13-21
Philippians 3:7-21
Hebrews 11:8-16, 24-38
1 Peter 1:3-9

Two Masters? Won't Work!

"No one can serve two masters. Either he will hate the one and love the other, or he will be devoted to the one and despise the other. You cannot serve both God and Money" (Matthew 6:24).

A S JESUS COMES AFTER OUR HEARTS HERE, WE ALL NEED TO PONDER his words and ask ourselves some questions. What occupies my mind? What concerns me? How impressed am I by what is new, better, "cutting edge," prestigious? When I think about security, is my focus on God or money? What has a greater hold on my life, God or money? Do I love using money to be merciful, to help others find peace with God? What does the evidence say?

Beware!

Because of the emphasis on money in the world all around us, materialism can creep into our hearts. It's not that our world doesn't have values; it has money as its value, and there are plenty who preach that value to us. But Jesus says take your choice—"you cannot serve both God and Money."

"*A root of all kinds of evil.*" That's what the love of money is. If we are eager and driven to gain more of it, we will stray from the faith and be "*pierced with many griefs*" (1 Timothy 6:10). There are some warning signs for us to be aware of in our lives. Have you said these things to yourself? "If I work one extra hour, I'll have more money for the bills." Then, "Just one more hour won't hurt." "Maybe we could go out to eat." "A weekend? Well, maybe just this once. I hardly ever miss the worship service." Our perhaps we hold back from giving to God to save for a house. We can wrap up our materialism with righteous-sounding statements. "But we want to use the house for the Kingdom." Sure, houses can be used for God, but check your heart. Are you trusting God can provide it without you having to back off your commitment to him?

It is not always the most spiritual decision to go without certain things. It is not unspiritual to buy things or to own a home.

The heart is always the issue. Disciples must live within their means and be content with what they have. They must realize that materialism is not the only "money problem" we face. When we are anxious and worried about bills and our financial situation, who is more the Master: God or Money? If you are looking for an example to follow, how about this one from Paul: *"I have learned the secret of being content in any and every situation, whether well fed or hungry, whether living in plenty or in want. I can do everything through him who gives me strength"* (Philippians 4:12-13). There is a man who served God, not money.

Missing a Miracle

An example of the opposite heart can be found in Judas—one of Scripture's most tragic characters and a classic example of someone who tried to serve two masters. He followed Jesus and masked his own love for money in Kingdom-sounding statements. In John 12:4-6 we find Judas expressing concern for a waste of money that could have gone to the poor, when in fact he was stealing money for himself. The hold money had on Judas' heart eventually led to his betrayal of Jesus and the taking of his own life. The the love of money was much deeper than his love for God and yielded bitter fruit.

After Jesus' resurrection, the guards responsible for securing his tomb went to report what had happened to the chief priests and elders. In turn the elders gave the soldiers a large sum of hush money and ordered them to say that the disciples stole the body of Jesus (Matthew 28:12). They stood in the very presence of the greatest miracle the world has known and missed it. . .all because of a love for money. But are some of us missing God's miracles for the same reason?

What is our sell-out point? 1 Timothy 6:17 tells us not to *"put our hope in wealth, which is so uncertain."* But wealth can "seem" so certain and bring such a sense of security and comfort. Having money can give us a sense of confidence and happiness. These are all feelings which can blind us to our true need for God.

Keep It Out!

I know a man who lost his very successful job. This caused him to dig deeper into his character and ask some hard questions. I saw in him an openness toward God and a humility about his life.

Several years later his success returned, and with the success returned his old self-reliance. Aware of the false security of wealth, Jesus tells his disciples in Mark 10:24 how hard it is for the rich to enter the Kingdom of God. 1 Timothy 6:11 instructs us to flee from the love of money and *"pursue righteousness, godliness, faith, love, endurance and gentleness."* Our confidence and hope cannot be in both God and money.

I can remember when we decided to leave the United States and move to the Middle East. Selling and giving away all our possessions was very freeing. We went with virtually nothing and spent three years not acquiring anything as we moved from the Middle East to Thailand and back to the Middle East. It was great to experience life in third world countries and realize how little I really need. Upon moving back to the U.S. it has been amazing how quickly materialism creeps in. Wanting comfort, desiring things. I need to consistently ask, what are the desires of my heart?

"Keep your lives free from the love of money," says the writer of Hebrews. When you have to keep something out, it must be trying to get in. Be determined to keep it out. Write out your own attitude toward money. Read it to some other disciples. Get their input about your statement and your life. Take it seriously. We cannot serve two masters. We must choose to honor God with our money, not despise God with it.

LAURIE TRANCHELL
Boston, Mass.

FOR FURTHER STUDY:

Matthew 28:11-15
John 12:1-6
Acts 5:1-10, 16:16-22
1 Timothy 6:3-19
Hebrews 13:5

From Worry to Wonder

"So do not worry, saying 'What shall we eat?' or 'What shall we drink?' or 'What shall we wear?' For the pagans run after all these things, and your heavenly Father knows that you need them. But seek first his kingdom and his righteousness, and all these things will be given to you as well" (Matthew 6:31-33).

W<small>E LIVE IN AN AGE TYPIFIED BY STRESS AND ANXIETY.</small> W<small>E HAVE</small> more tools, but less time. We have many "experts," but few examples. More sophistication, less satisfaction. Worry saps our energies and strength and enthusiasm like a 20th century plague.

Yet, worry is nothing new. It's been around for thousands of years. As always, Jesus has the solution for all of mankind's problems. In this passage, which could be entitled, "How to stop worrying and start living," Jesus gives us the solution to the age-old problem of worry.

Prescription for Worry

I can imagine Jesus, sitting on a mountainside with the crowds all around. They are listening intently to this Galilean with his strange teaching. Jesus sees the people, their faces drawn and haggard from the trials of their lives. He knows their thoughts. He knows their hurts, their tragedies, their turmoil. He glances up, and points to a flock of birds flying overhead. "Look at them," he cries out. "Doesn't God take care of them? Don't you think you are more important to God than a bird?" He sweeps his hand toward a field behind him. "Look at the lilies of the field. They won't be here long, but see how beautiful they are! Don't you understand God's care for you is so much greater?"

Jesus is not trivializing the cares of the people of his day. This is not a "Don't worry, be happy" philosophy of negligence and irresponsibility. Jesus is teaching the crowds to remember who is in control, and how much he cares for them. The message is still true today. God knows what we need! Will we, as his disciples, trust this message, or will we live like the "pagans"—using up all our best energies as we fret over things that are beyond our control?

Jesus' admonishment to cease from worrying carries with it two pieces of practical advice: 1) Trust in God, who cares for you, and 2) seek God's Kingdom and righteousness. The problem of worry cannot be resolved until both aspects of the solution are carried out. It's not enough just to set the mind and say, "Okay, I won't worry anymore; I'll trust in God." True peace and freedom from anxiety come only when the second part of the command is carried out as well. Followers of Christ must understand that their thoughts, their energies, their dreams and hopes are to be wrapped up in building up the Kingdom of God, and in becoming more like Jesus. And just in case the listeners want to put off this teaching until another day, he reminds them that today is what counts, today is what really matters.

The command comes with a promise: God will give you what you need.

Accepting the Cure

Worry can be defined as anxiety, distress, uneasiness, a troubled state of mind. This is not exactly a pleasant state of being. It is encouraging to me to realize that God does not want me to live this way, but desires that I have peace of mind and tranquility.

"But who can blame me for worrying about the economy, the pollution, the racial problems and the never-ending list of world problems?" we protest. And on a more personal level, "What about my job, my broken down car, my overdue rent, my teenagers?"

Or, "When will I ever (you fill in the blank): get married...get a boyfriend. . .have a child. . ." As disciples, it is easy to slip into the trap of worrying about when we'll be fruitful or become leaders.

I can be a "worry-wart" by nature, struggling with anxiety. I'll never forget the time several years ago when my husband was out of town and I was at home alone with two small children. As I crawled into bed, I prayed about the house's security and our safety. Then, as I lay there in bed, the fears began to creep in. Did I lock the basement door? That window at the back of the house isn't very secure. What was that noise? Isn't that the third time that car has driven past? On and on this continued, my prayers interrupted constantly by my fears. At some point during the night I realized what I was doing: To whom was I praying? If I truly believe in a God who cares for my every need, why was I so worried? I felt convicted that I could be praying and worrying at the same time and resolved to surrender my anxieties to God.

Too many people live in regret over the past or worry about the future. Jesus teaches us not only to trust in a loving God, but also to live in TODAY. "Don't worry about tomorrow," he says. This doesn't mean that we can't plan or dream about the future. Jesus knows that the only thing that we can really deal with is this day. It's important that we train ourselves not to bind up our energies with worries, but do all we can do today to serve him and his Kingdom.

Make a decision to cut worry out of your life. As situations arise that cause you concern, pray about them and entrust them to God. Trusting in his guidance and care, ask God to help you do all you can to help the situation. If there is nothing you can do, leave it in his hands, being assured that he is in control. If there is something you can do, then take action, today!

Resolve never to even say the words "I'm worried" unless you are confessing it as sin before God. If you are a "worrier," as all of us are at some time, be assured that you can change and be a man or woman with peace of mind.

Our world will not get any easier to live in. The problems we face daily will not usually get smaller, but larger. Age brings with it greater challenges, new things to worry about. As Christians, we are blessed to have as our God, a Father—a committed, all-powerful Father who cares for us and wants to carry our burdens. Let us be distinctive in the world as people who trust in him and seek to serve him. Let us show the world that there is a God by the peace that lives in our hearts. Let us change our worry to wonder—not wondering **if** he is in control, but having a sense of wonder because he **is** in control.

KAY McKEAN
Boston, Mass

FOR FURTHER STUDY:

Psalm 34
Romans 8:28-39
Philippians 4:4-7
1 Peter 5:5-7

Priority

First...the Kingdom!

"But seek first his kingdom and his righteousness, and all these things will be given to you as well" (Matthew 6:33).

J ESUS' SERMON REACHES A CRESCENDO. "FIRST...THE KINGDOM!" Now EVERYTHING changes. Everything must be re-examined. Everything must be re-scrutinized. Everything must be re-considered. EVERYTHING! Every dream, every plan, every desire, every use of money, every use of time—everything must have a Kingdom-first focus. It's no longer what self wants, now it's what God wants. It's no longer what builds me up the most, it's what builds God's Kingdom and God's people up the most. It's no longer "Where can I be most comfortable?" Now it's "Where can I be most effective?" Now, it's "How can I be most used?" not "How can I be most happy?"

New Dreams

Before becoming a disciple, my goal was to become a success-ful lawyer. I dreamed of financial wealth and security. I planned to own a prestigious home and to drive only the best of cars. I wanted to have a mountain retreat for weekend get-aways. I dreamed of writing books and living in warm climates. I was a relatively moral, non-confrontive, quiet kind of person. One of my greatest fears in life was public speaking because I was consumed with wondering what others were thinking about me. I was the typical "seek first myself" and "seek first the world" kind of guy. But becoming a disciple radically changed my whole approach towards life. I had to re-plan and re-dream my life so that it had a Kingdom-first emphasis and focus.

I don't believe that every disciple will change professions or that every disciple will sell all his possessions or that every disciple will move far away from his home and family. I do believe every disciple must seriously consider these possibilities and must be absolutely willing to do these. Certainly, a true Kingdom-first attitude always brings radical results. Everything is to become prioritized in relationship to the Kingdom immediately—our education, our professions, our family, our relationships, and our recreation. At baptism the process begins—the Kingdom-first perspective that will forever shape our lives must no longer be theory but practice. Our lives are to be consumed by the Kingdom. The Kingdom is to be our passion more and more. The Kingdom is to be our love more and more. The Kingdom is to be our life. Question: How can everything you previously planned, dreamed, and desired automatically become God's will for your life? Question: How can your pre-Kingdom plans automatically be Kingdom-first plans when you never considered the Kingdom before? Obviously they can't be! Then, how can a person's life be so much the same in goals, passions, desires and dreams? Obviously, again, they can't be. It all has to do with having, or not having, a "First...the Kingdom" heart.

How to Tell

How can you tell when you are *not* seeking first the Kingdom?

(1) When you don't have daily time with God in prayer and Bible study. (2) When your basic responsibilities to the church are a struggle and not a joy. (3) When special church events (retreats, devotionals, workshops, etc.) feel like a burden instead of an opportunity and a privilege.

(4) When you are not happy or not consistent in giving what you promised to God either in weekly contribution or in special missions contributions. (5) When you don't automatically give more when you are blessed with more. (6) When the greatest issues that help determine your life-decisions are personal comfort, personal desires, family concerns, money offers or worldly prestige.

(7) When you can't find the time to effectively share your faith and study the Bible with people. (8) When you gain greater feelings of accomplishment and satisfaction serving the financial kingdom, the educational kingdom, or the professional kingdom as opposed to God's spiritual Kingdom. (9) When you have a greater regard and protection concerning your personal schedule than you have in protecting the Kingdom schedule.

(10) When discipleship times, family night times and devotional times with your spouse and children are not both bonding and spiritually challenging times shared consistently together. (11) When

your talents and gifts get used in the world while only the leftovers go into the Kingdom. (12) When there is a greater demonstration of your leadership capabilities in the world than in the Kingdom.

(13) When gaining one more thing is of greater value than gaining one more soul. (14) When your dreams center more in this world than in the Kingdom. (15) When you feel greater excitement, happiness, challenge and thrill in the world than in the Kingdom of God.

Honestly, are you seeking first the Kingdom? Is your life consumed by the Kingdom and sold out for the Kingdom? The Kingdom life is filled with worship services, special spiritual enrichment programs and activities, long and loving fellowships, discipling times, winning as many as possible, serving brothers and sisters in Christ, helping the poor and needy, personal Bible study and prayer. But this is not simply a life of appointments and responsibilities—it is a purposeful, joyful lifestyle designed to aggressively spread the Kingdom of God around the world. The Kingdom consists of people who are volunteer soldiers in a battle between good and evil. The Kingdom is an imperialistic army bent on conquering every nation for the glory of our God. The Kingdom is made of sacrificial warriors persuading, pleading, and urging all in their path to follow King Jesus and to unite together in his glorious Kingdom. To serve wholeheartedly in this spiritual army must be our commitment, our dream, our goal, our desire, our passion, our pleasure—our life. Deep in our hearts there must always abide an intense desire that daily demands, "First. . . the Kingdom!"

RANDY McKEAN
Boston, Mass.

FOR FURTHER STUDY:

Matthew 22:34-40
Acts 20:24
Romans 12:1-2
Philippians 3:7-11

A Two-by-Four in the Cornea

"Do not judge, or you too will be judged.... You hypocrite, first take the plank out of your own eye, and then you will see clearly to remove the speck from your brother's eye" (Matthew 7:1-5).

"**I**T'S NOT MY FAULT." "MY PARENTS RAISED ME THAT WAY." "WHO are you to tell me that?" "I couldn't help it." "I wouldn't have done it if. . . ." "Why me?" "It's her fault." Sound familiar? We haven't changed much since the beginning in the Garden when our forefather Adam fell into sin and replied to God, *"The woman you put here with me —she gave me some fruit from the tree, and I ate it"* (Genesis 3:12). "Don't blame me—it's not my fault" has become the battle cry of the modern age.

We crave a scapegoat for our problems and discomfort. Children blame parents; spouses blame each other; employees blame employers; society blames present political administration; present political administration blames previous;and on and on.

Ridiculous!

In the midst of our situation, Jesus calls for an end to blame-shifting and a return to personal responsibility. As Jesus taught in Matthew 7:1-6 we must learn to confront the "planks" in our own lives in order to become like him and impact the lives of others. Stop for a moment and see the picture Jesus paints. A man with a huge plank of wood protruding from his eye is trying to help a man with only a speck of sawdust in his eye. An outrageous sight! Hilarious! Jesus had a sense of humor that evoked an image of sheer ridiculousness—yet our interactions with others are often just that ridiculous to God. Instead of admonishing one another (Colossians 1:28-29) and building each other up through construc-tive challenges (Ephesians 4:29), finger pointing becomes a weapon to divert attention from ourselves. Criticalness and defensive reactions mask the true source of the problem—that is, our own guilt. We fear being open with our lives and letting our true selves be identified and corrected to become more like Jesus.

This character sin affects us in each of our relationships, but none more profoundly than in marriage. This is something we've had to work through in our marriage. Our pattern consisted of one of us expressing hurt feelings, the other having a defensive, prideful reaction whereupon the finger was pointed back. Then we both would retreat from each other without resolving anything. Thank God for discipling and the help of others in our lives! Other married disciples have helped us in such incredible ways to work through these worldly patterns and move on to great victories. The call is for each of us to look honestly and humbly into the mirror of our lives and apply Romans 12:3, "...*Do not think of yourself more highly than you ought, but rather think of yourself with sober judgment, in accordance with the measure of faith God has given you.*"

Jesus talks about removing the plank from our eye so that we then can remove the speck from our brother's eye. Jesus expects us to help one another and to be in others' lives. Watch out for two extremes: (1) Becoming inwardly focused, seeing only our problems, and then letting insecurity and selfishness keep us out of others' lives; (2) Trying to help others straighten out their lives without being open to the same help ourselves. Such hypocrisy will keep us from making anything but another hypocrite. Jesus calls us to look at ourselves first, but not stop there. We are called to repent first ourselves and then be ready to help our brother or sister.

A Sober Estimate

Do you have a sober estimate of yourself? Are you quick to blame-shift? Are you critical of others, not easily finding the good that they do? How do you respond when challenged? Jesus is calling each one of us to be truthful, humble servants for him.

You may be saying now, "How do I get a sober estimate of myself?" "How do I see myself for who I really am?" "How do I stay humble before my brothers and sisters—not being the one to throw stones?"

First, look daily into the mirror of God's Word. The Bible speaks to us and, if we listen with humble hearts, it shows us who we really are. How ridiculous to look in a mirror and forget what you look like. In the same way, how foolish to look in the Word of God and not let it transform your life (James 1:22-25). Let God's Word speak to you!

Second, pray fervently for God to open your eyes and give you insight into your heart and life. Pray to see yourself the way that God sees you. Pray for a readiness to see the good in others. Psalm 139:23-24 is an incredible prayer to cry out to God: *"Search me, O God, and know my heart; test me and know my anxious thoughts. See if there is any offensive way in me, and lead me in the way everlasting."*

Third, be open with those in your life. Be quick to confess your sin (James 5:16) and your temptations as well. Don't let critical thoughts or attitudes linger in your heart; immediately get them out.

Finally, have a humble attitude toward challenge in your life. Be grateful that God has put people in your life that love you enough to speak the truth in love to you. Be eager to take the initiative to ask for input and correction even before it is given to you. Let Psalm 141:5 be your goal: *"Let a righteous man strike me—it is a kindness; let him rebuke me—it is oil on my head. My head will not refuse it."*

Make decisions today to take the plank out of your eye. Then experience the joy of having clear spiritual vision and being able to love and help people without hypocrisy.

ANDY AND STACI YEATMAN
Milan, Italy

FOR FURTHER STUDY:

Genesis 37-45
Psalm 51
Matthew 18:21-35
1 Corinthians 15:9-11
Philippians 2:5-11

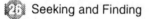

How Much More

"Ask and it will be given to you; seek and you will find; knock and the door will be opened to you. For everyone who asks receives; he who seeks finds; and to him who knocks, the door will be opened. "Which of you, if his son asks for bread, will give him a stone? Or if he asks for a fish, will give him a snake? If you, then, though you are evil, know how to give good gifts to your children, how much more will your Father in heaven give good gifts to those who ask him!" (Matthew 7:7-11).

G OD WANTS TO BLESS US. HE HAS A MAGNIFICENT PLAN TO BLESS US. He is the one who is most disappointed when we do not get blessed. But he forces his good gifts on no one. He waits for us to ask.

"Ask," "seek," and "knock" are all action verbs. So often, God is ready to give us total victory and all he wants is for us to take the first step: ASK! Consider three ways we should be asking:

Asking God for the Right Questions

Many times, when bad things happen to us, we ask, "O Lord, why me?" When things don't go as well as we would like them to go, we ask, "Why are things so bad?" We never get an answer to the first question, and if we do get an answer to the second one, we find things continue to go badly anyway. Here is a vital thought: Those questions that do not solve problems are the wrong questions. We need to ask God to help us answer the right questions— ones that will empower us: "What can I learn from this problem?" or "What can I do to change this situation?" "What is your will for my life?" When our ministry is not doing well, what kind of questions are we asking ourselves? When our marriage is not doing well, are we asking, "What can my husband/wife change that will make my life easier?" or are we asking, "What can I change that will make his/her life and our marriage better?" Jesus teaches us to ask the right questions that will lead to actions and thereby solutions to life's many problems. There are some questions God is eager to answer. What questions are you asking?

Asking God for "Good Gifts"

We have two beautiful daughters. Like many fathers, I can't wait to give them the best of just about anything (when we can afford it, of course). God is our Heavenly Father, and he is more than eager to give us the best. The Bible teaches, *"You do not have, because you do not ask God"* (James 4:2). Why don't we ask God? Sometimes we don't think we are worthy. Sometimes we let our sinful past influence how we look at ourselves. This may have been Judas' problem. Perhaps he couldn't bring himself to ask for forgiveness. The truth is that we who are disciples are pure and blameless in God's eyes because of Jesus. Sometimes we do not ask because our faith is weak, and we are not confident about the "much more" of the Heavenly Father. We aren't sure about what is true—namely that God loves nothing more than giving good gifts to his children.

At other times, we don't ask because we don't know what we want. This is the most difficult situation for God. Don't you hate it when someone is being indecisive? Do you know how you want your personal ministry to grow in the next two months? Do you know what you want to change this month? Do you know which brothers or sisters you want to help into leadership? Decide what you want and then ask God!

Asking with Trust in God's Perfect Answers

Jesus here symbolizes the good gifts of God as bread and fish. When looking at the first reference of stones and bread in verse 9, it can be read referring to our "needs." There is a saying that "Life is tough." It is, but do we maturely accept it? So many times we think we are getting "stones"—all the bad breaks, the difficult disciples, the unconquerable circumstances. So we become resigned that God has somehow given us these stones to grind our teeth on instead of the "bread" that will meet our needs. We set ourselves on *survival mode* through the tough times. Recovering from my first delivery, I (Jane) lay in bed just focusing on the pain and discomfort of having a baby. I felt only the stones in my life. A sister pointed out that I did not radiate with joy. After all, this was our first baby! How right she was. I had forgotten about the bread—the joy that God has given us through the life of a beautiful baby. How easy it is for us to forget that God is meeting our needs by giving us bread that will fulfill our needs as disciples of Jesus. Has God given you "bread" only to have you call it a "stone"?

When we were in Hong Kong, we dreamed of planting a church in mainland China, but there was a need for us to go to Taipei, Taiwan. Our first reaction was not of great joy but of disappointment. It meant that we would not have the glory of going into Communist China to preach the Word. I realized how deceived and wrong my motive was although the dream was a great one. God had exposed my heart. When we set our hearts on fishing for God, he put a great desperation in us for the lost in Taipei. Are you asking for your own glory or God's? What a difference it makes. In one case we come up empty. In the other we are richly blessed.

STEVE AND JANE CHIN
Taipei, Taiwan

FOR FURTHER STUDY:

Isaiah 65:24
Matthew 14:15-21
Mark 11:22-24
John 15:7-16

Building with Gold

"So in everything, do to others what you would have them do to you, for this sums up the Law and the Prophets" (Matthew 7:12).

C AN THE ENTIRE REVELATION OF GOD PRIOR TO THE COMING OF JESUS possibly be summed up in one sentence? Jesus himself says it can, and today that one sentence is well known as the Golden Rule. We need to know it like we know John 3:16 or Luke 9:23. It needs to be part of us—in our minds and in our hearts.

Jesus Lived It

From birth to death Jesus fulfilled this scripture. His standard for treating others was not how they treated him. Daily he put others' needs before his own. He didn't have to become a man; he didn't have to be humiliated, spat upon, mocked or killed, but he knew others needed for him to experience those things. Throughout his life he demonstrated incredible compassion as he touched a leper (Matthew 8:3); healed many (Matthew 8:14-17); broke social and racial barriers (John 4); showed firm compassion to a woman caught in adultery (John 8:3-11); noticed an individual woman's suffering even in a crowd (Luke 8:47); and even called the little children to him (Luke 18:16). Throughout his entire life he put the needs of others before his own. He thought, "How would I want to be treated?"

In the end Jesus laid down his life for all to be saved. He totally fulfilled the Golden Rule. Being innocent, he carried our guilt. As Philippians 2:3-5 says, "*Do nothing out of selfish ambition or vain conceit, but in humility consider others better than yourselves. Each of you should look not only to your own interests, but also to the interests of others. Your attitude should be the same as that of Christ Jesus. . . .*"

Jesus walked with his disciples for three years, not to teach them theology, but rather to teach them a lifestyle of putting others first. He told them, "*Love one another. As I have loved you, so you must love one another"* (John 13:34). His life was a constant demonstration of his message. This cohesive life and doctrine altered the disciples' behavior and attitudes permanently.

We Must Live It

The world teaches, "Do to others before they do to you." "Look out for number one." "Don't let anyone hurt you or take advantage of you." Jesus taught just the opposite, and he led the way.

Jesus taught radical concepts: turn the other cheek; go the extra mile; love your enemies; pray for those who persecute you; forgive; give to the needy in secret; be a servant to all. Through this transformation of heart and attitude we will have life and have it to the full (John 10:10).

To please God and to be Christ-like we must die to worldly self-protective and self-centered thinking. We can't say, "Until my needs are met, I am going to hold back on giving my all." Take a moment to meditate on what others have done for you. Memories flood my mind:

- Praise God for those who have cared enough to confront our sin, enabling us to change.
- Thank God for a forgiving spouse!
- To God be the glory for so many who have served us when we needed them!

In our family we truly saw a testimony of love during Kelly's mother's battle with cancer. For a six-month period she struggled with the illness, the chemotherapy and being eight hours away from Kelly.

During this time Kelly went to be with her one week out of every month. The love and care of our brothers and sisters was a blessing to us. The church's leadership provided us with spiritual direction and emotional support. Disciples called her frequently to pray with her. Many wrote letters and cards and sent scriptures. Some helped around the house with special meals or other needs. After death came, a special disciple took a week of her vacation to drive Kelly to Maryland and help her pack her mother's house. Brothers drove down with Javier to load the moving vans and drive them. Many others drove three and a half hours to a memorial service out of state!

During a challenging time, we were encouraged and strengthened by disciples who practice the teaching of Jesus. We were the "others" they "did unto." Our lives were blessed in the receiving; their lives were blessed in the giving.

This principle of Jesus is powerful, but we need to get practical about making it part of our lives. Here are some suggestions to get you started:

(1) Make a list of specific times when someone has met your physical, emotional and spiritual needs. Remember how you felt.

(2) Think of the needs of others around you right now. Think of both Christians and non-Christians who are sick, have a sick child, are elderly, are lonely, need someone just to listen. Think of those who are in sin, discouraged, struggling with praying, need a hug, have a physical ailment, need a baby-sitter or whatever the case may be. Think of your husband, wife, children, roommates, neighbor, work mate, etc.

(3) Put yourself in their shoes. What would you want others to do for you? How would you want them to treat you?

(4) Now do it. Just do it! "Do," says Jesus. Don't just think, "Do."

(5) Next turn the coin over. Think about ways you don't want people to treat you—how you don't like to be talked down to, how you don't like someone to repeat what you shared in confidence, how you don't like people to criticize you behind your back. Think about other things like this.

(6) Don't do these things. Just don't treat others in ways you don't want to be treated.

(7) Maintain a grateful heart and attitude toward God and others for all they have done for you. Keep meeting others' needs without looking for praise or recognition.

When we live like this, we build on the foundation of Jesus Christ with "gold," not with hay or stubble (1 Corinthians 3:12). Test this kind of life by fire and it is proven genuine every time. And to God be the glory!

JAVIER AND KELLY AMAYA
Brookline, Mass.

FOR FURTHER STUDY:

Isaiah 61:1-6
Matthew 25:31-46
Philippians 2:3-4
James 1:27
1 Peter 5:2-5

Part 4

Discernment

One-Lane Road

"Enter through the narrow gate. For wide is the gate and broad is the road that leads to destruction, and many enter through it. But small is the gate and narrow the road that leads to life, and only a few find it" (Matthew 7:13-14).

"This is good and pleases God our Savior, who wants all men to be saved and to come to a knowledge of the truth" (1 Timothy 2:3-4).

S EEMINGLY CONTRADICTORY STATEMENTS. ON THE ONE HAND God says that he wants all men to be saved. We like this statement; it makes us feel warm, safe, accepted and loved by God. It fits our picture of God as a grandfather, rocking in his chair, beckoning us to come be with him. But then there is the stark statement of Jesus, God in the flesh, that says only a *few* will find the road that leads to life. "How unfair," we think. Why would God, who wants all men to be saved, make the road that leads to him so narrow that only a few find it?

Because Only a Few Search

This statement is part of the conclusion to Jesus' sermon. He begins with the Beatitudes, says that Christians are to be the light of the world, and warns against legalism. He then teaches personal responsibility for anger, lust, marriage, vows to others, retaliation, loving our enemies, meeting the needs of the poor, prayer, money, worries of this life and criticalness. And then he says , "This is the only way to God; don't be fooled." Our first thought? This seems impossible!

Many agree that this is the most difficult teaching of Jesus. It is certainly one of the most misunderstood and emotionally rejected of Jesus' teachings. Our tolerant world thinks the narrow road is fanatical. But you cannot in any way be faithful to Jesus' message and teach anything but a narrow road. Go through life thinking the road is broad and wide and you certainly will not be on the road to life, or most importantly, you will not get to the end of it.

God certainly wants all men to be saved. That is why he sent a son who spoke so clearly and plainly about what it takes. Going the way of the broad road rejects God's wisdom and his love. It rejects Jesus' sacrifice on the cross. It says, "I know better than God what life and eternity are all about. I don't need narrow-minded advice from anyone for my life. I'll do it my way!" Watch out! The Bible warns that on the broad road you will face terrors and traps of many kinds (Proverbs 4:10-19, 15:10, 21:16).

On the broad road are so many people, with so many standards (none with God's standard) all going so fast—the noise is deafening—all rushing like lemmings over a cliff, heading for eternal destruction (Matthew 25:46).

"But small is the gate and narrow the road that leads to life, and only a few find it" (Matthew 7:14). Jesus described perfectly the path for us and then he walked on it in front of us, leading us! God's wisdom in living color! But *"only a few find it."* The fact is that only a few search. Only a few are willing to go wherever it leads. But everyone who wants it and seeks it, will find it (Matthew 7:7-8). Yes, it's narrow. No, it's not impossible to find! If you don't want it, there is no way you will find it. If you eagerly seek it, there is no way you can miss it! Yes, the road is narrow, but it is wide enough to handle every person who wants nothing but to do the will of God.

Staying on It

While Kim was a medical laboratory technician, she worked with many patients who had received pancreas and kidney transplants. These patients were excited about their transplants; for them it meant a second chance in life. They were required to take pills every day to prevent their bodies from rejecting the transplant. There were some who took their pills faithfully for a while, then stopped. They became increasingly ill, and when their blood was tested, it showed their bodies were destroying the transplanted organ. These people had forgotten how fragile their transplanted organs were. They began to feel better and think the pills were not so important; after all they "felt" fine. The sad ending for a few was that they did not get another chance.

As with the transplant patients, we too were given a second chance when we decided to walk that narrow road with Jesus. However, finding the narrow road does not guarantee that we will go through the final gate. Once we have found the narrow road, we must faithfully continue on it. Just as the organ transplant patients needed to take their pills every day to protect their new lives, we must make daily decisions to stay on the narrow road all the way to the end. Consider a few:

- The decision to stay humble (Luke 18:17).
- The decision against materialism and desires of this world (Luke 18:24-25).
- The decision to persevere through hardships (Acts 14:22).
- The decision to stand firm in our convictions through persecutions (Luke 21:12-19).
- The decision to believe and obey God whatever the circumstances (Hebrews 3:5-19).

As you consider the narrow road today, just be grateful you've found it. Be grateful Jesus opened it up for you. Be grateful his sacrifice has taken away the sin that blocked your way to it. Be grateful he sent someone to show you clearly where it is and how to walk on it. And then be determined. Be determined to stay on it. Be determined to help others find it. But whatever you do, never apologize for it. It is the road to life!

DEAN AND KIM FARMER
Berlin, Germany

FOR FURTHER STUDY:

Psalm 119:1-8, 29-32
Isaiah 5:1-30
Mark 10:17-31
Luke 14:25-33

Not Always What It Seems

"Watch out for false prophets. They come to you in sheep's clothing, but inwardly they are ferocious wolves. By their fruit you will recognize them. Do people pick grapes from thornbushes, or figs from thistles? Likewise every good tree bears good fruit, but a bad tree bears bad fruit. A good tree cannot bear bad fruit, and a bad tree cannot bear good fruit. Every tree that does not bear good fruit is cut down and thrown into the fire. Thus, by their fruit you will recognize them" (Matthew 7:15-20).

W E ARE FRAGILE. AND LIFE AS A DISCIPLE OF JESUS IS FULL OF potential danger. We walk daily through a spiritual minefield, our souls always susceptible to the spiritual threats that surround us. Watch out disciples! We live in a world filled with religious people who seem to be as passive and gentle as the sheep they outwardly imitate, but are actually ferocious wolves on the inside. These wolves are capable of real harm to God's flock, but you would never be able to tell by their exterior.

It wasn't just Jesus who warned the disciples about the perils of the masqueraders. The apostles Paul, John and Peter also told Christians to *"be on their guard..."* against false teachers, false brothers, fake friends and the like. There are numerous passages in the New Testament which warn the reader *"not to be deceived."* It is only through the Word, the help of brothers and sisters, a humble heart that says "God, search me and know me" that you can come back to reality. Our enemy is experienced, hardened, creative and the father of lies. We must heed Jesus' warnings and be prepared for such a wary opponent or we too will become deceived.

The Test of a Heart Is What It Produces

"By their fruit you will recognize them" (v.16, 20). Not by their words but by their actions. Not by their proposals but by their results. Not by their declarations but by what they produce. The test of a man's heart is what he does: the combination of actions and attitude. Jesus calls it his *fruit*. The visible result of the power within his soul. Jesus taught that what comes out of our mouths is what overflows out of our hearts (Matthew 12:34). He taught that

it is the content of our hearts that determines our actions and therefore makes us spiritually *"clean"* or *"unclean"* (Mark 7:17-23). There is no way around it. What our lives in Christ produce speaks volumes about the content of our hearts.

Bad Fruit Means a Bad Heart

The teaching of Jesus is easy to understand. It is refreshingly clear. Bad trees always produce bad fruit. There are no exceptions. Shallow hearts produce shallow disciples. Hypocrisy multiplies hypocrisy. Impure hearts produce doomed disciples. Criticalness spreads like a virus from heart to heart. Faithlessness topples cold heart after cold heart like dominoes in a row.

Jesus told his disciples to *"Watch out."* Be care-ful and care for the hearts of the people you know. Remember: appearances deceive. We must be looking past the appearances and into the lives of those with whom we have contact. Bringing a disguised wolf into the fellowship of sheep is a spiritual nightmare. A wolf among the sheep will do harm to many and will not be happy until he has killed some.

How can we get over being so naive when it comes to the people around us? We are so willingly deceived at times, especially by people who seem friendly or religious. The solution is simple if we apply Jesus' teaching. We must have a deep conviction that the only true way to discover what is in someone's heart is to apply the Word of God to his or her life and look at the fruit produced.

Until someone sits down and studies the Bible it is impossible to know what kind of heart they have. Many fine *appearances* have crumbled when confronted with the Bible's teaching about discipleship, repentance, salvation and the true church. It is sometimes shocking to see what we thought to be *nice* people react so pridefully or defensively to the Word, yet you must understand that it is God, through his Word, showing the tree by its fruit. Others, however, that looked to be *too prideful* or seemingly less likely to respond well to the message of Jesus have radically changed when confronted with the Word. The point is that we never can know with certainty what will be inside the heart of our fellowman until we open the Scriptures together and the Spirit of God cuts and convicts. The bad fruit of mockery, defensiveness, pride and self-pity are just a few of the signs of a bad heart. Watch out!

No Fruit Means a Bad Tree Too

A fruitless tree is a useless tree. This powerfully clear teaching of Jesus appears time and again in the New Testament (see

Matthew 3:10, 13:22; Luke 13:6-9, 19:11-27; John 15:2, 6; Hebrews 6:8). Jesus warned the chief priests and the Pharisees that *"the kingdom of God would be taken away from you and given to a people who will produce its fruit"* (Matthew 21:43).

This concept is understood once you understand the following: In the Christian life there is no neutrality of example. We are either good examples or we are bad examples. There is no such thing as a neutral example. Just as there is no such thing as a neutral husband, a neutral father, a neutral friend, there is no such thing as a neutral Christian. Either we bear good fruit for the glory of God, or by not bearing fruit we show our hearts for what they are: sterile and barren. A disciple who bears no fruit is an example of faithless Christianity, of mere religion. We cannot forget that it was Jesus who said, *"Every tree that does not bear good fruit is cut down and thrown into the fire"* (v.19).

Good Trees Are Full of Good Fruit

All disciples should produce fruit of all kinds as a testimony to the power of God's Spirit at work in their hearts. The religious world goes round and round debating whether the Greek word used here for fruit *(karpos)* means the fruit of the Spirit (Galatians 5:22-23; Ephesians 5:9), or the fruit of making other disciples (Matthew 28:19, John 15:16). Why on earth should it be either/or? Disciples should produce fruit. Period. Fruit of the Spirit in characters that are transformed into the image of Christ, and the fruit of disciples that are to God's glory as we reproduce ourselves spiritually in others. There's no option to work on one or the other. It's a total effort to produce as much as possible of both. A good heart refuses to get entangled in the semantic debate and simply desires to produce what God has made it capable of producing: good fruit. Every kind. As much as possible.

What kind of fruit does God see in your life?

ANDREW GIAMBARBA
Miami, Florida

FOR FURTHER STUDY:

N.T. warnings:	Teachings on fruit:
Acts 13:40	**Psalm 1:3, 92:12-15**
1 Cor. 3:10, 6:9, 10:1-6	**Jeremiah 17:5-8**
Galatians 6:7	**Ezekiel 47:1-12**
1 Thess. 5:19-22	**John 12:24; 15**

Far More Than Words

"Not everyone who says to me, 'Lord, Lord,' will enter the kingdom of heaven, but only he who does the will of my Father who is in heaven. Many will say to me on that day, 'Lord, Lord, did we not prophesy in your name, and in your name drive out demons and perform many miracles?' Then I will tell them plainly, 'I never knew you. Away from me, you evildoers!'" (Matthew 7:21-23).

B Y THE TIME WE GET TO THIS POINT IN THE SERMON, THIS JESUS statement should not surprise us. He means for us truly to make him "Lord" and to actually do the will of his Father just as he did. He means for us to do this until the very end. But it must be easy to have an initial flush of excitement about following Jesus only to slip into something that falls far short of the real meaning of Lordship. It must be easy because so many do it.

"Communism didn't die, it just grew old," said a sullen government official during the Soviet Communist Party's demise. Communism did die, but it died *because* it grew old. It became bloated and burdened with age. It didn't suddenly fall. It crumbled beneath the weight of disinterest and lost values. It lost the edge and excitement of life. A few short generations after its birth, it's gone.

In the 20th century alone, we have witnessed the rise and fall of many great movements. But are God's people exempt from such "falls"? We must face the reality of what may easily happen to us if we allow our love for God and our commitment to his Kingdom to "grow old." All along the journey, we must examine our lives and ask whether we have become bloated and burdened in some kind of spiritual middle age. In short, we need again to ask ourselves, "Is Jesus really Lord?"

Unlikely Examples

What does it mean to say that Jesus is Lord? Perhaps we should ask the centurion in Matthew 8, who spared Jesus the effort of going to his home. *"Just say the word,"* he replied, *"and my servant will be healed."* This man understood the authority of lordship. Just say the word. He had a job, community responsibility and, most likely, a family. Just say the word. He had hundreds of men depending upon his leadership. Just say the word. Is that your heart with God? How about the word, "go" as in, "Go and make disciples"? Do you still say to Jesus "Just say the word"? When was the last time you actually studied the Bible with a friend and saw him/her become a disciple? Or have you become too busy, too self-absorbed, too much wanting someone else to go and do the work for you? How about the word "give"? Do you weary of missions contributions? Do you think more about how you really do need that new car or TV or stereo? After all, "We have to take care of our kids now that we are older." The centurion understood the authority of Jesus and was commended for his great faith. So, too, we should hear Jesus say the word and respond with the faith of this great man.

In Matthew 15 we read about a woman who knew Jesus was Lord. She came to Jesus, knelt at his feet and begged him to help her. She had a daughter who was ill and only Jesus could help. It did not matter that she suffered inconvenience or even insult. Her daughter was sick and only the Lord could heal her. She recognized his sovereignty. Too often, when things do not go our way, we give up and quit. We become fatalistic, believing more in the whims of circumstance. The demons of doubt and self-pity destroy our faith. This woman would not take "no" for an answer. Jesus was Lord. He could save her daughter. And she would not quit until she received from the Lord what she came for. She knew the Sovereign Lord could do whatever he wanted to do. She needed only to impress him with the importance of her request. When was the last time you asked Jesus to do the impossible in your life? When did you last get down on your knees and beg the Sovereign One to grant your request? To change your character? Heal a friend? Save the soul of a loved one? Do we live as those who realize the amazing sovereignty of Jesus our Lord?

Jesus or "The Good Life"?

As we grow older, there is a longing for comfort, ease and security. We begin to think more of our family and providing the "good life" for them. We are less apt to take risks or even make sacrifices. We become more measured and lose the radical commitment we first had when we agreed to follow Jesus. We wouldn't think of leaving the church. We may still be leaders. Yet, in the very words of Jesus, we are "evildoers" if he is no longer the Lord for whom we will go anywhere or do anything.

I know what I speak of because I am challenged by these same thoughts and feelings in my own life. Several years ago, I left my law practice (at the height of my career), took my family and trained for full-time work in the ministry. We moved to Asia, learned a new language, adapted to a different culture and were exposed to countless tropical diseases. Our six-year-old son suffers from a rare digestive disorder, and we nearly lost our two-year-old daughter to a collapsed lung. We moved to six different cities in three different countries in less than four years. My parents kept our home address written in pencil. We saw the churches we led grow and prosper. We also felt the loneliness of defeat. Just recently we returned to America to fill a new role in God's Kingdom. But guess what? The siren's call of comfort beckons me at every corner. It seems so easy to conform to the patterns of this world. Yet, if I want to make it to heaven, I must continue to deny myself, take up my cross and follow Jesus as my Lord. God's not interested in my resume, but my heart.

Are you part of the movement of God in our day? Have you seen some exciting things? Will it be just another movement on the ash heap of history, or will we continue to forcefully advance his Kingdom in our generation? Will we allow our lives to grow old and meaningless; or will we, like Caleb, cry out with our hearts aflame for the hill country of youth? It is the battle that makes a warrior young. Do you heed the words of your commanding officer? Only then is Jesus truly Lord!

JOHN BRINGARDNER
Los Angeles, Calif.

For further study

Matthew 8:5-13,18-22
Matthew 15:21-28
Matthew 17:1-8
Matthew 19:16-30
Revelation 3:14-22

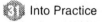

Be Wise—Build Right!

"Therefore everyone who hears these words of mine and puts them into practice is like a wise man who built his house on the rock. The rain came down, the streams rose, and the winds blew and beat against that house; yet it did not fall, because it had its foundation on the rock. But everyone who hears these words of mine and does not put them into practice is like a foolish man who built his house on sand. The rain came down, the streams rose, and the winds blew and beat against that house, and it fell with a great crash" (Matthew 7:24-27).

WITH THESE WORDS, JESUS CONCLUDES THE SERMON ON THE MOUNT. The essence of all that he taught on this famous occasion is contained here, because the Word of God gives us everything that we need for life and godliness (2 Peter 1:3). Whether we are dealing with the development of actions or attitudes, we find the answers in the Bible. As with most of Jesus' teaching, this section is simple and profound at the same time. To seek first the Kingdom, we must grasp and live the principles contained in this closing section. What are the lessons which Jesus intended to impress upon our hearts?

Expectations

One, he expected people who had any interest in being wise to listen to his words. The problem in our world today is that the Bible is more readily available but less read than at any time in recent history! Since Jesus has promised to judge us at the last day by his words (John 12:48; James 2:12), ignorance is anything but bliss! Reliance on the teaching of religious groups or the ideas of men in general is dangerous beyond description. Only those who dig into the Bible are building the right foundation for time and for eternity.

Two, Jesus intends for us to act on these words once we have heard them. Knowing without doing is worse than not knowing in the first place (Luke 12:47-48). To hear the Word without obeying is to be self-deceived (James 1:22-25)! By definition, a disciple is a learner and a follower. One without the other will not fulfill the expectations of Jesus for our lives.

Three, the storms of life are a reality. Both the wise and the foolish men in the account experienced about the same things by way of trials. Actually, the disciple will have more trials in one sense because of persecution brought on by virtue of his devotion to Jesus! Thankfully, he will have less trials in another sense because he will escape the damage brought on by the rampant sin which character-izes the lives of non-disciples. But storms he will face! The "believe and get rich" message comes from false prophets . The implication that following Jesus will eliminate all or most of life's problems is damaging to the faith of those who accept such a message. Follow-ing Jesus can hardly result in a life which is substantially different from the one he experienced (read John 15:18-20).

Four, the type of value system we adopt for the foundation of our lives will be ultimately revealed. We may look good when the storms are absent, but our hearts will eventually be revealed by the storms of life. Jesus did not discuss the *storm* of life, but rather the *storms* of life. Whether you make it past all of the storms depends totally on the strength of your foundation, which is your faith in Christ (1 Corinthians 3:11). It may take many years and many storms to fully reveal the nature of your faith, but both God and Satan will make sure that it is revealed. Thankfully, God has promised that we will not be tempted beyond our ability to endure if righteousness is our highest goal (1 Corinthians 10:13).

Evaluation

At this point, some questions about your foundation are in order. Do not pass over them quickly, because it is easy to be self-deceived.

1. How excited are you about studying the Word of God? (Is it a matter of simply having a quiet time, or do you really hunger and thirst for the Word?)
2. Do you make use of driving time and other times to listen to tapes and read spiritual books?
3. Are you more diligent about study now than when you were a young Christian, or less diligent?
4. Does the word obedience produce a positive or negative reaction in your heart when it is men tioned in a sermon or lesson? (In other words, does it make you think about burden or blessing?)
5. Are there areas in your life where you know you should be doing things differently, but are sim-ply not carrying through? (See James 4:17.)
6. How do you view trials in life — as though God

were failing you or as though God were
maturing and helping you?
7. Do you find yourself questioning God very
   often or even getting disappointed or angry
   with him?
8. What would it take to make you fall away from
   God and his church? (Think long and hard
   about your answer to this one because Satan
   knows the answer already!)

Decision

This section of Scripture is concerned not so much with
growth in character development, but with decision! Jesus is
putting the two choices of life and death before us—the choice of
the narrow road or the broad road. Nothing in between exists. We
are either on one or the other. We are either hot for him or we are
lost, because lukewarm is actually worse than being cold (Revelation 3:15-16)! It is time to evaluate our spiritual lives with the
above questions in response to Jesus' Sermon on the Mount, make
some firm decisions, and then develop a plan to immediately put
those decisions into practice.

When Jesus, God in the flesh, finished this sermon, the people
who heard it were amazed (Matthew 7:28-29). However, as we
continue reading Matthew's account, we find that some were moved
by their amazement to truly follow Jesus, while many others did not
make the kinds of decisions which were life changing on a long-term
basis. The sermon is now over. You have looked at its demands and
its promises. It is time for your response. Are you amazed? More
importantly, will you remain amazed with the Son of God and his
words? May he give you the convictions and the power to say and
live "First...the Kingdom!" And to him be the glory!

GORDON FERGUSON
Danvers, Mass.

FOR FURTHER STUDY:

Psalm 119
Romans 5:1-5
Hebrews 12:1-15
James 1:2-12

A Colony of Heaven

W E HAVE BEEN TO THE MOUNTAIN TOP. WE HAVE SEEN HOW LIFE can be. We have seen a world where people are humble— where they learn from one another and open their lives up to whatever God wants. We have seen a world where people are committed—committed to showing mercy, making peace, and enduring ugly opposition with grace and even joy. A world where ordinary people become extraordinarily distinctive and, like salt and light, have extraordinary impact.

We have seen a world where heart is more important than performance, where being technically right is not nearly as important as being inwardly right. A world where people want to resolve every conflict, forgive every wrong, love every enemy. A world where no one cares about getting the credit, where things done in secret bring even more satisfaction than things announced in the headlines.

We have seen a world where God rules—where his Kingdom has come into the hearts of people and where doing his will is really all that matters. A world where people are not anxious because they are confident about the "much more of the Heavenly Father."

We have seen a world where people are interested not in judging one another self-righteously but in helping one another grow. A world where people find the greatest value in spiritual possessions not in those things that will fade and perish. A world of builders whose foundations are solid and whose work endures through all that life throws at them.

The Impossible Dream?

It seems to me that there are fundamentally three responses one can have to all that Jesus says in this message.

1. "No way! Who could possibly do this?" Here is the person who looks at the Sermon on the Mount and says, "Give me a break. You don't really expect people to live like this do you? It's too hard. No one can do it. Trying will just make you feel guilty." This answer is heard not just from the man in the street, but from prominent psychologists who say Jesus had no right to place such heavy demands on people.

2. "It's wonderful. We should think more about it." I knew a man once who preached a sermon on this sermon of Jesus'. In it he spoke of "The Man from LaMancha" and the well-known song from that Broadway musical that talks of those who will "dream the impossible dream," and he preached that in this sermon that's exactly what Jesus was calling us to do—to go after the impossible. This man's sermon was masterfully constructed and delivered in dramatic fashion with a mesmerizing rhythm and cadence. After he preached it, there were those who wanted to hear it again, and eventually he was asked to come and deliver it in other churches. Then civic clubs invited him to share it, and colleges extended invitations. Someone kept up with how many times he gave it. I wouldn't be surprised if some kind of record was set. Just recently, now many years after he first gave it, I heard he was still getting requests for it. People like the nobility of the Sermon on the Mount. Its message touches something deep inside us. In one major European country it is still highly esteemed as a philosophy of life, although few in that country attend any church. But while there are many who like to hear it played like some fine piece of chamber music, there are few who want to live it (see a similar problem in Ezekiel's day in Ezekiel 33:31-32). But Jesus said it would be this way: *". . . small is the gate and narrow the road that leads to life, and only a few find it."* The world Jesus describes in this sermon will be found by only a few. Many will admire it from a distance, praise its grandeur and majesty; few will enter it.

3. "It's a great challenge, but it's God's will and I want it." Those with this spirit will become a world within the world—a colony of heaven on a troubled planet. They will become a world of faith in the midst of doubt—a world of hope in the midst of despair—a world of love in the midst of hate. "The few" who are in this new world will make more difference than all "the many" put together.

For years in the United States we have had big sweepstakes in which one person wins as much as $10 million spread over thirty years. I would presume there are such contests in other countries as well. Those who want to have an opportunity to win, dutifully send back as many as four replies. Many will enter. Only a very few will win. While one can send back his cards to make sure he is given a chance, the final outcome is out of any hopeful's hands. All one can do is wait for that phone call. For most it never comes.

Fortunately, this is not the way you find yourself in God's "few." Yes, *many* will miss it. Yes, only a *few* will find it. But it is entirely up to you and me. We can become part of those few in this brave new world. There's no lottery with God. We can commit ourselves to this sermon and the Lordship of the one who spoke it. It's our choice. In one sense this sermon is "The Impossible Dream." No one can live it without error, but all those who put their hearts into it and go for it and go for it and go for it, will, by the grace of God, start changing their part of the world.

Make a Decision

Make a decision that you want in your life *every* attitude and *every* action described in this sermon. Do that today. Do it tomorrow. Do it forever. Don't sing the praises of this sermon. Put into practice its words. Get help. Get lots and lots of help. A person with the first three beatitudes in his or her heart wouldn't think of going it alone. Be totally committed to every principle, but be totally open about every struggle you have with obeying.

Finally, be confident. Be confident you can live these words in any circumstance. I have multiple sclerosis. But that's no excuse. What's your excuse? There is no good excuse. I can live by these words in my circumstance, and you can live by them in yours. Be confident that *with his help* you can do exactly what he planned for all of us to do when he went up on a mountain side, sat down and taught us *". . . Seek first the kingdom of God. . . ."*

T.A.J.

Reminders

On the following pages you will find some short thoughts from the articles you have just read designed to provide quick reminders of the heart of this powerful sermon. Pick these up from time to time to regain your focus. Let them remind you of your need to go back and reread entire articles. Use them to help you be faithful.

W e can get out of our sin and have our need met only through confession and humility—only by owning up to where we really are and what condition we are really in. But once we do that, how things change. Suddenly those who are beggars have everything. Theirs is the Kingdom of God!

THOMAS A. JONES
1 Poor in Spirit

◆

W e have hurt our Father, and when that realization touches our hearts, we want desperately to change from inside out and from top to bottom. That is repentance.

SHEILA JONES
2 Mourning

Meekness is built on great faith, for the meek person looks outside himself for the power to live. Because he is totally open to God, he is confident that God will work in all things for his good.

GORDON FERGUSON
3 Meekness

◆

As we feast on the Word of God, we will also hunger to please him, to obey him, to become more and more like him. This desire to please him will find a direct application in loving others as he does. Jesus hungered to serve others, to even give up his life for them. The things of God are all about serving and saving others for the glory of God.

THERESA FERGUSON
4 Hunger

Getting into someone else's skin. Feeling what they feel. That's really what mercy is all about. What would it be like for us to be the other person in a given situation?

ERICA KIM
5 Mercy

◆

The Word is what purifies us. It discerns the thoughts and attitudes of our hearts. It will diagnose us and sanctify us. In Psalm 119:9 David says we can keep our hearts pure by *"living according to [God's] word."* David did more than snack on the Scriptures, he made sure they were his steady diet.

EMILY BRINGARDNER
6 Pure in Heart

Jesus never compromised his mission or his purpose. Whether he was rested or tired, encouraged or discouraged, praised or despised, he was always ready to help others make peace with God. Jesus, **the** peacemaker shed his blood so we could have peace. And he calls us to die to ourselves so others can be made right with God.

LYNNE GREEN
7 Peacemakers

◆

Only in the role of warrior, then, can we begin to understand why Jesus dares to say, "Blessed are those who are persecuted." It is like saying, "Blessed are the fighters, the people of courage who choose to fight Satan's opposition rather than run."

SCOTT GREEN
8 Persecution

It was with this background of Old Testament significance that Jesus used salt to describe the spiritual identity of his disciples. He calls us to be the preservors of righteousness in the midst of godless lifestyles. To be the "conspicuous character that brings out the best" in human nature in contrast to so much that show man's worst.

WYNDHAM SHAW
9 Salt of the Earth

◆

There is nothing more useless and frustrating than a burned out light bulb. It is counted on, yet unavailable. Is your light counted on, yet unavailable or is it a beacon for the lost world?

JEANIE SHAW
10 Light of the World

Perhaps you make deals with yourself: "Today I don't need to share my faith because I studied my Bible extra long this morning." What good lawyers we can be! The religious world is full of lawyers. They aren't fulfilled, though, and they're certainly not happy. Joy comes when we trust and obey. There's no other way!

DOUGLAS JACOBY
11 Righteousness

◆

Failing to resolve things with a sister or brother will erode our relationship with God. Our worship is not pleasing to God. So if this is your situation, "leave your gift"—that is, sort things out as soon as possible!

VICKI JACOBY
12 Reconcilation

Here Jesus says to throw away your checklist Christianity. One can pass many of our little status checks and still be far from God. . . . Jesus certainly doesn't say to disregard the absolute lines God has drawn because those lines give us boundaries, but boundries without the heart make a hollow shell.

AL BAIRD
13 Absolute Purity

◆

One man—one woman—one lifetime. God's way works! Complete faithfulness in marriage. Go in the front door of marriage and keep the back door shut. Go in with a mindset of giving of yourself, of meeting his or her needs, of working through conflict, of staying **put** through the rough times, of not giving up.

GLORIA BAIRD
14 Marriage

Our religious lies, like the Jews, are generally not blatant. And yet how easy it is for us to exaggerate the facts for our benefit. How smoothly we slide into deceit that conveniently leaves something out. We have stopped running the race and bought into the death trap of the father of lies (John 8:44).

JIMMY & ANITA ALLEN
15 Truthfulness

◆

Jesus' teaching that one should carry the baggage not only the first mile but a second as well surely was a shock to those who heard it. This was a radical sermon! Jesus was saying go beyond what is required by the authorities. Certainly the spirit of Jesus' message condemns *any* resentment we may feel against a legitimate authority.

DOUG WEBBER
16 Second Mile

Regardless of how much we may love the brotherhood, any bitterness or resentment in our hearts towards our persecutors simply reduces us to the level of the world. Shall we conform to the hearts of wicked men? Shall we follow in their footsteps? After Jesus' costly sacrifice on the cross, have we still learned nothing?

MARK REMIJAN
17 Loving Enemies

◆

God gives because he wants to. Do you give in secret? How many times have you felt hurt or even struggled when your giving was not acknowledged? Are you content when no one but God sees your sacrifice? Do you give without wanting anything in return and lend without expecting to be paid back (Luke 6:30)?

PATSY REMIJAN
18 Giving to the Needy

How deeply do you wrestle with God through life's disappointments, hurts and tragedies? Do you call out to God with loud cries and tears as you learn submission through times of challenge and suffering? We must never let religious words and actions characterize our prayer life. Remember, do not be like the hypocrites. Instead, be real with your God.

ADRIENNE SCANLON
19 When You Pray

◆

Fasting tests our earnestness to move God to action, forcing us to admit that sometimes prayer alone may not suffice (Mark 9:29). God desires to humble us, not to beat us down, but in order to lift us up. He wants us to learn the power of discipline and self-control, and become truly spiritual.

BRIAN SCANLON
20 When You Fast

J esus makes a strong case here that it does not make sense to be consumed with treasures here on earth because they will not even last here.
In contrast to fading earthly treasure is our salvation which never spoils or fades.

BOB TRANCHELL
21 Treasure

◆

B ecause of the emphasis on money in the world all around us, materialism can creep into our hearts. Its not that our world doesn't have values; it has money as its value, and there are plenty who preach that value to us. But Jesus says take your choice—you cannot serve both God and Money.

LAURIE TRANCHELL
22 Money

Resolve never to even say the words
"I'm worried" unless you are confessing it as sin before God. If you are a
"worrier," as all of us are at some time,
be assured that you can change and be
a man or woman with peace of mind.

KAY McKEAN
23 Worry

◆

Serving wholeheartedly in this spiritual army must be our commitment,
our dream, our goal, our desire, our
passion, our pleasure—our life. Deep
in our hearts there must always abide
an intense desire that daily demands,
"First...the Kingdom!"

RANDY McKEAN
24 Priority

Make decisions today to take the plank out of your eye. Then experience the joy of having clear spiritual vision and being able to love and help people without hypocrisy.

ANDY & STACI YEATMAN
25 Judging

◆

Those questions that do not solve problems are the wrong questions. We need to ask God to help us answer the right questions—ones that will empower us: "What can I learn from this problem?" or "What can I do to change this situation?" "What is your will for my life?"

STEVE & JANE CHIN
26 Seeking and Finding

Jesus walked with his disciples for three years, not to teach them theology, but rather to teach them a lifestyle of putting others first. He told them, *"Love one another. As I have loved you, so you must love one another"* (John 13:34-35).

JAVIER & KELLY AMAYA
27 The Golden Rule

♦

Yes, it's narrow. No, its not impossible to find! If you don't want it, there is no way you will find it. If you eagerly seek it, there is no way you can miss it! Yes, the road is narrow, but it is wide enough to handle every person who wants nothing but to do the will of God.

DEAN & KIM FARMER
28 The Narrow Way

We must have a deep conviction that the only true way to discover what is in someone's heart is to apply the Word of God to their life and look at the fruit their heart produces.

ANDREW GIAMBARBA
29 By Their Fruits

◆

Will we allow our lives to grow old and meaningless or will we, like Caleb, cry out with our heart's aflame for the hill country of youth? It is the battle that makes a warrior young. Do you heed the words of your commanding officer? Only then is Jesus truly Lord!

JOHN BRINGARDNER
30 Not Everyone

The type of value system we adopt for the foundation of our lives will be ultimately revealed. We may look good when the storms are absent, but our hearts will eventually be revealed by the storms of life.

GORDON FERGUSON
31 Into Practice

◆

Those who say, "It's a great challenge, but it's God's will and I want it" will become a world within the world—a colony of heaven on a troubled planet. They will become a world of faith in the midst of doubt—a world of hope in the midst of despair—a world of love in the midst of hate. "The few" who are in this new world will make more difference than all "the many" put together.

THOMAS JONES
Epilogue

Coming Soon
from
Discipleship
PUBLICATIONS INTERNATIONAL

Raising Awesome Kids in an Awful World
by Sam & Geri Laing

Mind Change: The Overcomer's Handbook
by Thomas Jones

The Servant King
A Quiet Time Book for Children
Volume 2 Kingdom Kids series
by Clegg & Betty Dyson

She Shall Be Called Woman
Volume One
Edited by Linda Brumley and Sheila Jones

God and History
An Old Testament Overview
By Gordon Ferguson

Daily doses of power

Thirty Days at the Foot of the Cross edited by Tom and Sheila Jones. Powerful devotional readings showing how the cross applies to thirty different areas of our lives. First released in August, now in a 2nd edition--paperback format. From teens to those in the Kingdom many years, the feedback has been overwhelming. A book you will go back to again and again.

$4.99 (# 200061)

Discipleship Publications International
1 Merrill Street
Woburn MA 01801

Call 1-800-727-8273 for credit card orders

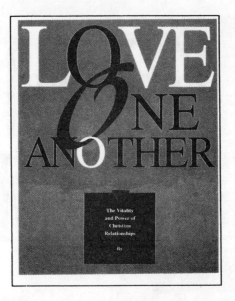

"Follow Me"

Powerful Women Living from the Heart

Two great tape series

More Than Conquerors
$12.95 (#8190)

Crashing Through the Quitting Places
Lisa Johnson
Putting Insecurity to Death
Joyce Arthur
No More Unnecessary Guilt
Kay McKean
What the Bible Says About Confidence
Joanne Webber and Gloria Baird

Matters of the Heart
$12.95 (#8191)

My Heart's Desire
Elena McKean
Do Not Let Your Heart Be Troubled
Pat Gempel
Encouraged in Heart
Kay McKean
What the Bible Says About Forgiveness
Theresa Ferguson and Jeanie Shaw

Discipleship Publications International
1 Merrill Street
Woburn MA 01801

Call 1-800-727-8273 for credit card orders